At Issue

Human Waste

Other Books in the At Issue Series:

At Issue

I Human Waste

Ronald D. Lankford Jr., Book Editor

GREENHAVEN PRESS
A part of Gale, Cengage Learning

GALE
CENGAGE Learning·

Detroit • New York • San Francisco • New Haven, Conn • Waterville, Maine • London

Elizabeth Des Chenes, *Managing Editor*

For more information, contact:
Greenhaven Press
27500 Drake Rd.
Farmington Hills, MI 48331-3535
Or you can visit our Internet site at gale.cengage.com

LIBRARY OF CONGRESS CATALOGING-IN-PUBLICATION DATA

Human waste / Ronald D. Lankford, Jr., book editor.
    p. cm. -- (At issue)
    Includes bibliographical references and index.
    ISBN 978-0-7377-5896-2 (hardcover : alk. paper) -- ISBN 978-0-7377-5897-9 (pbk. : alk. paper)
    1. Sewage disposal. 2. Feces. 3. Sewage--Industrial applications. I. Lankford, Ronald D., 1962- II. Title. III. Series.
    TD730.H86 2012
    363.72'88--dc23

                  2011028023

Printed in the United States of America
1 2 3 4 5 6 7 15 14 13 12 11

Contents

Introduction

Americans, Europeans, and many people around the world take modern sanitation for granted. Most people in developed countries have at least one bathroom in their house that is connected to a septic or sewer system. These people express little concern over the possibility of sewage or human waste contaminating the local water supply; they know that a local sanitation plant will cleanse the sewage of any unhealthy bacteria. For these people, clean bathrooms and sanitation are just facts of life.

Neither bathrooms nor sanitation, however, are universal. In reality, 2.6 billion people, or over 25 percent of the world's population, have no bathroom facilities or even access to restroom facilities. In rural areas and cities, in refugee camps and public housing, many people are forced to relieve themselves in nearby alleys, in a convenient bush, or, for many, openly in public. Unfortunately, using the local alley for a restroom is more than inconvenient and embarrassing: it also creates the potential for a massive health crisis. Every year millions of people die from feces-related diseases. Rose George, the author of *The Great Necessity*, noted in an interview, "The death toll from diarrhea, which is largely caused by poor sanitation, is astronomical. It's the second biggest killer of children in the world after respiratory diseases."[1]

The crisis is not easily resolved. Modern sewer systems and sanitation plants are expensive, and in rural localities, familiar habits are difficult to change. A number of organizations and individuals, however, are working hard to resolve the crisis by bringing sanitation and clean water to all of the world's residents.

One popular method utilized by a number of world organizations in recent years has been Community Led Total Sanitation (CLTS). As the name implies, this method actively involves the community that is being served, as opposed to only installing toilets or other sanitation devices and expecting the local people to use them properly. CLTS strives to educate local populations, understanding that unless the entire village or town or community participates, it may continue to experience problems related to an unprotected water supply.

CLTS was developed by Kamal Kar of India. Kar partnered with the organization Water Aid in March of 2000 to bring clean sanitation to a village in Bangladesh. Once the program had been tested in one village, Water Aid brought the program to four hundred villages in northern Bangladesh over the next three years, offering improved sanitation to over sixteen thousand families. Kar notes:

> The needs of the community must be foremost and the facilitators should work according to them. The solidarity of the community and the idea of people helping each other are very important. Village leaders and teachers must be involved and fully informed from the outset. Everything should, of course, be done at the convenience of the community and not the facilitators.[2]

Recently, the United Nations Children's Fund (UNICEF) developed a CLTS program in Nkhata Bay in Malawi, Africa, bringing toilets to rural villages like Chikwina. In the past, residents of the village simply relieved themselves in the nearest bush or cover. After the arrival of the UNICEF program, villages began learning basic hygiene skills, such as washing one's hands with soap and water after using the restroom. UNICEF also encouraged the village to build rudimentary toilets, explaining that open defecation was causing cholera outbreaks. "We agreed with what the health officials said," one villager noted. "One person would be upstream defecating, while another would be collecting drinking water downstream, not knowing the water was contaminated."[3] By making these changes, villages like Chikwina quickly improved the health and well-being of its residents.

Because sanitation problems differ from one country to the next, organizations have relied on a variety of programs. In India, for instance, many people have toilets in their homes. Public sanitation, however, has remained a problem. It was estimated that as many as 660 million people in India, or 55 percent of the nation's population, continued to defecate in public in 2009. Part of the difficulty has been created as millions of rural dwellers moved to urban centers. As a result, the sheer number of people has overwhelmed available facilities.

To address this issue, Rajeev Kher started Shramik Sanitation Systems in 1999. Unlike many organizations that operated on a nonprofit status, Kher's project was a business. Kher's humanitarian goals, however, mirrored the work of many charities:

> We wish to ensure that each Indian has access to a clean restroom, and to provide our cleaning technicians with a sense of dignity about their work, which people in the sanitation business currently lack. This is our main challenge. Not only are we looking at portable restrooms, but providing sanitation to everyone. We use the profits generated from our paying work to provide portables in the slums, as well as at public events.[4]

By the end of 2010, Shramik had installed twenty-four portable toilets, which the company continues to service. When asked about his plans for Shramik over the next three to five years, Kher replied:

> We wish to provide more than a million services per week catering to slums, construction sites, disaster management, street (pay-for-use units), tourism and school sanitation. We're also moving into waste management, including disposal and treatment of waste to form energy. We'll even be developing low-cost package treatment plants to offer a 'Total Sanitation' solution.[5]

The efforts that are being made by Water Aid, UNICEF, and Shramik in India, Bangladesh, Malawi, and other countries have brought sanitation and improved health to thousands of people. These efforts have raised awareness worldwide, helping to draw a connection between proper sanitation and public health. The struggle to reach the 2.6 billion people without proper sanitation, however, is only beginning. Millions of people live in remote villages that are difficult for relief efforts to reach, and many others remain resistant to change. Finding a way to fund projects that will educate and provide everyone with adequate sanitation will remain a central goal for governments, businesses, and world organizations in the near future.

Notes

1. Katharine Mieszkowski, "Let's Talk Crap," *Salon*, October 16, 2008. www.salon.com/books/int/2008/10/16/big_neces sity.
2. Kamal Kar, "Subsidy or Self-Respect? Participatory Total Community Sanitation in Bangladesh," IDS Working Paper 184, September 2003. www.communityledtotalsanitation.org /sites/communityledtotalsanitation.org/files/wp184_0.pdf.
3. Gospel Mwalwanda, "Unicef Promoting Use of Toilets in Nkhata Bay," *Nation*, April 18, 2011. www.nationmw.net/ index.php?option=com_content&view;=article&id;=17929: unicef-promoting-use-of-toilets-in-nkhata-bay&catid;=27: development&Itemid;=22.
4. Mary Shafer, "Promoting Portable Sanitation in India," *Pumper*, October 2010. www.pumper.com/editorial/2010/10/ promoting-portable-sanitation-in-india.
5. Shafer, "Promoting Portable Sanitation in India."

1

Human Waste: An Overview

Rose George, as told to Katharine Mieszkowski

Rose George is a British journalist. Katharine Mieszkowski is a senior writer at Salon.

In an interview with Salon, *Rose George explains that improper sanitation is creating a growing, worldwide health crisis. Over 2.5 billion people have no sanitation, which means that they neither have access to a toilet nor live in a community with a wastewater treatment system. As a result, untreated sewage is often filtered back into the local food chain and water system, causing deadly diseases and diarrhea. Unfortunately, few people have been willing to speak openly about these health risks because of the subject matter. Starting in the 1950s in the United States and Europe, modern sanitation practices have added decades to lifespans in those regions. George also notes that sanitation practices vary around the world and that countries like Germany are exploring more ecological ways of processing sanitation.*

If you're one of those Americans who does not leave the house without showering and applying deodorant, you may be surprised to learn that hundreds of millions of people around the world likely think that you're unclean, if not downright disgusting.

It's all about how you clean your butt.

In cultures that use water to clean down there after defecating, dry toilet paper as a substitute is something of an ass

Rose George, interviewed by Katharine Mieszkowski, "Let's Talk Crap," *Salon.com*, October 16, 2008. This article first appeared in Salon.com, at Salon.com. An online version remains in the Salon archives. Reprinted with permission.

abomination. Yet to those of us raised on Charmin, using a bidet, even though it's more hygienic, is just as foreign.

Bathroom hygiene is just one of the foul and frankly fascinating aspects of what's euphemistically known as "sanitation," which British journalist Rose George explores in her new book, *The Big Necessity: The Unmentionable World of Human Waste and Why It Matters*.

For her reporting, George ventured into the bowels of London's sewer system with an emergency breathing apparatus strapped on her waist. She squatted in a doorless public toilet in China. And she visited slum dwellers in Mumbai [India] who live in areas with 100 public toilets for 45,000 residents.

Ninety percent of the world's sewage ends up untreated in oceans, rivers and lakes.

Here in the industrialized world, where we happily flush it and forget it, it's hard to imagine that literally billions of people elsewhere have no access to a toilet. It may also be difficult to believe that 90 percent of the world's sewage ends up untreated in oceans, rivers and lakes, some of that filth burbling out of our supposedly sophisticated sewage systems. While the humble toilet has added decades to the lives of those of us lucky enough to have one, George reports, it's also created a whole host of environmental problems.

Salon talked toilet, latrine and bidet with George by phone from London.

[Katharine Mieszkowski:] *Some 2.6 billion people have no access to a toilet whatsoever, and that includes a latrine, a bucket or a box. They literally have nowhere to go. Can you talk about what that means?*

[Rose George:] Anyone who has traveled to India and taken an early morning train will know exactly what that means because all you have to do is look out of the window.

What you'll see is people just simply squatting there, doing their business where they can.

What it means in terms of public health is catastrophic. Human waste can be extremely toxic. It can carry millions of bacteria, viruses and worms. And you don't want that kind of stuff lying around. But these 2.6 billion people, who have absolutely no sanitation, have no choice but to use the nearest bush or roadside. That means it's being tramped around in the human environment. It's getting into people's food, it's getting into their water, and it's making them extremely sick.

The death toll from diarrhea, which is largely caused by poor sanitation, is astronomical. It's the second biggest killer of children in the world after respiratory diseases.

Why isn't this more of an international health issue?

It's quite simply that we don't want to talk about it. There is a linguistic problem. We don't have the language for it anymore because we've resorted to euphemism. In the West, we've been able to resort to euphemism because we have the wonderful flush toilet and waterborne sewage system, which gives us the luxury of being able to flush something away and assume it will be treated elsewhere.

We literally flush it out of our mind as well, and it's not in public discourse anymore. This wasn't always the case. Three hundred years ago it was considered an honor to attend kings when they were seated on their toilets. People in the West have this great system and I think they just assume that it's the same for everybody in the world.

Is there a celebrity out there who wants to be the Angelina Jolie of toilets, making this a popular issue?

Matt Damon has started to talk about school latrines, which is great news. It's inevitable because he does a lot of great work on clean water. For example, if you go to a school in a village in Africa, you've got a nice clear water supply, and you've got the nice tap, but you've got no latrines. So obviously the kids are going to be contaminating the water supply because they simply have no sanitation. You've got to make the connection. You can't have clean water without decent sanitation.

You found in your research there's no single solution. Why not?

The answer is not that everybody should have a sewer or everyone should have a toilet. That is simply impractical, and most countries can't afford it. Culturally, in sanitation, we're very different around the world. People have different attitudes to hygiene and toilets. Some countries are fecal-phobic and some countries are not. China is quite at home with excrement, and uses it as fertilizer, whereas Indians are not. They're quite averse to any use of human waste.

In Benin, Africa, some very interesting research was done into what would make people buy a latrine. Mothers, who didn't have a latrine, could see that their kids were getting sick every week with diarrhea. They were spending money on medicine, and their kids weren't going to school, but they still wouldn't buy a latrine.

An academic named Mimi Jenkins discovered that the biggest incentive for someone to buy a latrine in Benin was to feel royal, because the royal family had one. It was a question of pride and status, it wasn't about health. Health messages never work, because nobody wants to be nagged, even when they've got the evidence in front of them.

So telling people, "This is where the cholera is coming from," doesn't have as much impact as appealing to their pride?

Exactly. It's what I call the "doctors who smoke" understanding of people. Doctors who smoke know it's bad for them, yet they still do it. What a lot of sanitation activists are saying is that we have to make people want toilets. It has to be something they aspire to and desire.

Isn't part of that incentive making defecating in the outdoors unappealing?

Yeah, and there's a very interesting movement going on in many developing countries, including India, Cambodia and Bangladesh, called Community Led Total Sanitation. It appeals to people's sense of disgust.

A few visitors will go to a village, and the villagers will want to show off their village to the guests. They'll take them around the village, and then at the end of the tour, the visitors will say, "Well, yes, that's nice, but can we see your open defecation grounds?"

Because they're polite, the villagers will take them there. The technique is to make people stand there and confront it, to not be able to turn away from the fact that they're shitting in the open, and that their kids are tramping it back into the village, and that they're all eating it. Someone calculated that people in villages who are doing open defecation are probably ingesting 10 grams of shit a day. That's pretty disgusting.

People will run off and dig latrines. Once the whole village is cleaned up, nobody will want to be the dirty person in the village. And once the village is cleaned up, the clean village will be in competition with the next village, and that village will want to clean up. It's a chain reaction.

Don't some governments pay for latrines, and the people don't always use them?

Yes. For 20 or 30 years, India has been pouring money into sanitation, and has been building, or subsidizing, lots of extremely nice latrines all over the country. But because they're nicer than people's houses, they get turned into a temple, or an extra room, or a goat shed, or simply used for storage. Because people have this engrained habit of going out into the bush, they don't see anything wrong with it.

Well, if you're used to going outside, maybe it's kind of gross to go inside, in a bathroom, or even near your home.

That is a problem, and that's what makes sanitation very tricky. In India, it is considered unclean to have a latrine close to the home. The answer is to make sure that it is a decent latrine, and it doesn't smell. It has to be an adequate latrine, it has to have some kind of fly-proofing, and some kind of vent pipe so there is no odor. If it's a decent enough place, then people get used to it.

Let's talk about some of the slums you visited where there are 100 toilets for 45,000 people. What happens then? People don't end up using the toilet, right?

They use it if they can. But if it takes half an hour to get from one side of the slum to the other, or you're waiting in line and the doors are falling off, and it's unpleasant, then people won't use it. They just go in the street, or on the roadside, or they find the nearest beach. There are beaches in Mumbai that are absolutely filthy.

We should worship the toilet. It's been an enormous medical advance.

What are flying toilets or helicopter toilets?

A flying toilet is a plastic bag. You defecate into the plastic bag, you wrap the plastic back up, and you throw it. Hence it's a helicopter or flying toilet. This is the only form of sanitation available to a lot of slum residents in Africa, particularly in Kenya and Tanzania. At least it's potentially containing the toxic human excrement, but obviously it's not ideal, and they're all over the place in the slums. It's quite a nice phrase for an extremely unpleasant practice.

Isn't it true that your own shit isn't a danger to you, it's other people's?

If you wanted to, you could probably ingest your own shit, but it wouldn't necessarily be toxic. But the problem is that shit is such a good vehicle for disease transmission. That's why we in the West have such good sewer systems and waterborne waste treatment. In about 1850 or so in London, a doctor called John Snow realized that cholera was being carried in drinking water, and it was being carried in human shit.

By some accounts, the toilet has added 20 years to the modern lifespan, so this thing that we won't even discuss is actually responsible for perhaps decades of all of our lives.

Yes, exactly. Last year [2007], the readers of the *British Medical Journal* voted sanitation the biggest medical advance in the past 200 years. It is an amazing thing—the toilet. We do live longer because of the toilet. Before sewers and toilets became popular in the 19th century, one in two children in London died before their 5th birthday. There was an enormous mortality rate, and that dropped dramatically, especially when soap and hand washing also became popular. We should be on our knees before the toilet.

We should worship at it.

We should worship the toilet. It's been an enormous medical advance. It's been fantastic, so I think that we should give it its due.

Even in industrialized nations, where we have sewer systems, our bathroom habits vary widely. For instance, there are two main ways of cleaning your butt. Can you talk about what those are, and who does what?

The world divides into water cultures and paper cultures. This comes into quite stark relief in Japan because Japan used to be a paper culture. Two hundred years ago they used sticks or stones or paper. And now, because Japan has had a toilet revolution, they've turned into a water culture, and they have very high-tech toilets with in-built bidets and drying systems that can massage you and probably sing to you.

But the U.S. and the U.K. stubbornly remain paper cultures, and attempts to introduce bidet toilets have failed. Hygienically, bidet toilets are infinitely superior. Using toilet paper to clean yourself down there makes about as much hygienic sense as cleaning yourself with a towel and imagining you're rubbing off the dirt. We've got a very unhygienic way of cleaning a place of our body that we would like to be very clean.

Actually, we're pretty disgusting, and we just don't realize it.

We are kind of disgusting. I'm being polite about it. In water cultures like India, where you see all these people going to do their business with a little cup of water, they think we're extremely dirty. They can't believe it. Muslims, who have to be scrupulously clean according to the laws of the Quran, also think it's kind of weird that we have this habit of using paper, and imagining we're clean. We're not.

Can you talk about the attempt of the Japanese company Toto to bring bidet toilets to Americans?

In Japan, Toto is an enormous company, and it's one of the great names of Japanese industry, like Sony or Mitsubishi. More households have a Washlet toilet, which is a bidet toilet, than have a computer. They've had astonishing success in Japan, so quite reasonably they thought, "If we can do it in Japan then we can do it everywhere else," because Japan was also a paper culture.

So Toto USA started about 20 years ago and they've been trying to introduce the high-tech or high-function toilet over here. Americans really aren't that interested. The Neorest, which is this stunningly gorgeous toilet, the top-range Toto toilet, has been installed in various places, including one large casino hotel in Las Vegas. It's apparently popular with celebrities.

What are some of the features of one of these high-end toilets?

One of the basic features is the lid will lift automatically. It will deodorize the room. It has special dirt-repelling, extremely advanced chemicals layered on the ceramics. They all have a remote-control panel next to the toilet so that you can adjust the heat. All the seats are heated; that's just standard. Some of the toilets can check your blood pressure. Some can test your urine. Some of them can weigh you. They can play you music. You can plug in your MP3 player. I think the only thing they can't do is read to you.

There is so much technology fetishism in the U.S. about things like our iPhones, but we just don't seem to have much interest in innovations in toilets?

The way to convert someone to the beauty of a Washlet toilet is to use one. I've spoken to lots of people, Americans included, who have been to Japan, and they just go, "Oh God, yeah, the toilets are amazing." But because they're not the widely spread yet in the states, most people don't come across them.

So, we're just content with these high toilets, which actually physiologically are kind of impeding our normal bodily processes. You actually don't want to be seated high up on the toilet. That's not helping your evacuation processes.

Squatting is better for you?

Squatting is better. I'm not suggesting that we all go and get squat latrines. But certainly toilets in the U.S. are very high now because they're like thrones or chairs, and that's not the best physiological position.

What's the story with ecological toilets?

In Germany, ecological sanitation is quite popular, and one of the most common ecological toilets is called a urine-diverting toilet. It makes very good ecological sense because if you make sewage less liquid, it's much easier to treat afterward.

What happens with the urine?

You can just pipe it off somewhere else. It's a very good fertilizer. It contains a lot of nitrogen and phosphorous, so you can put it on your garden if you want to. The toilets require men to sit down to pee, so that is a bit of a stumbling block. But Germans do it.

There's also the composting toilet, which uses no water whatsoever. It used to be known as an earth closet. You just have a toilet and you add some kind of ash, or soil, and it just decomposes and it's apparently odor-free. You can use it in your garden if you leave it composting long enough. It should be perfectly safe and pathogen-free, but you have to do it properly. There are lots of composting toilets in America now. They're particularly useful in rural or mountain areas.

I spoke to an ecological sanitation professor in Norway—Norway is also very fond of ecological sanitation—and he said that he has a friend who has a composting toilet. He said the friend has a little girl who had obviously grown up using a composting toilet, and when she went to school and saw this normal water toilet she was freaked out. She said, "What is going on? There's all this water," and she couldn't believe it.

Because we have such water issues these days, we really do have to question whether throwing several liters of clean drinking water into a toilet, dirtying it and then spending millions and a loss of energy cleaning it again is really the best way to proceed.

Besides using water and energy, what are the other environmental impacts of industrialized sewage systems?

When human waste is treated it is separated into effluent, which is the cleaned liquid. Then it's put back into the water system, and what you have left is solids, or sludge. That's all the dirt that you've cleaned out of the sewage. In the states, the most common way of dealing with this is to apply it to land. It's been renamed "bio-solids," and it's applied to land all over the country.

There is an increasing activist movement which is very unhappy with bio-solids being applied to land. One of their concerns is that there are heavy metals in the sludge, because our sewer system is set up so that everybody can put anything down their toilets, or their sinks. A recent investigation found that it's common practice for hospitals to put their unused pharmaceuticals down the sink or down the toilet.

We don't know what's in the sludge; it can change from day to day. The people who are against sludge being applied to land say that, quite reasonably, until we know more about it, let's be more cautious. On the other hand, bio-solids proponents are saying it's perfectly safe, it's all regulated, the EPA [Environmental Protection Agency] thinks it is safe, so it's safe.

How have your own bathroom habits changed since you started researching this book?

I put the toilet seat lid down before I flush. When you flush with it open there is a very fine spray of whatever you've just flushed all over the room. So, I thought, well, I'll just put the lid down, and I've become a bit of a nag about that idea.

Otherwise, I do think about our sewers. You can find motorbikes down sewers. You can find hospital aprons or syringes. There are all sorts of chemicals and pharmaceuticals and storm water. Grit—anything that comes off a road and goes down a drain—ends up in a sewer.

So I really think about what I put down the drain. I won't put cooking oil down the sink anymore because I've seen congealed fat blocking a sewer. It was disgusting. It's just these enormous blocks of fat. That's what really disgusted sewer workers, more than excrement. They hate it. It gets into their pores, and it makes their lives extremely dangerous because they have to remove it. And it blocks the sewers. It's just a very bad idea. Restaurants are pouring used cooking oil down the drain but so is everybody. And so I've become a bit of a puritan about that. I will wipe it out of pans and pour it on the garden.

I wash my hands differently. I wash them a bit more and I wash my wrists as well, because that's in the CDC's [Centers for Disease Control and Prevention's] hand-washing guidelines, which are five or seven steps. But I also frown when I'm in a public toilet and people don't wash their hands. I give them looks.

2

Sewage Poses
Many Health Risks

American Rivers

American Rivers is an organization promoting conservation and healthy rivers that serve the broader community.

Despite environmental controls and treatment facilities, raw sewage continues to affect the quality of drinking water in the United States. Every year, thousands of people become ill as a result of waterborne pathogens caused by sewage. These illnesses vary from bacteria that cause mild diarrhea to viruses that cause liver damage. Other potentially harmful effects from raw sewage include toxic algal blooms and the effects of pharmaceutical compounds. It is important that federal, state, and local governments continue to properly fund and maintain sewer systems to assure that all Americans have access to clean, safe water.

Every year hundreds of billions of gallons of untreated sewage flow into our rivers, lakes, and coastal waters. Unknowingly, many Americans and their loved ones risk serious illness when untreated sewage seeps into the water they use for recreation or drinking. The EPA [Environmental Protection Agency] estimates that over 7 million people suffer from mild to moderate illnesses caused by untreated sewage every year. Another &12frac; million get seriously ill. However, the number of illnesses caused by raw sewage could be much higher than we think. Many people that get sick from untreated sewage aren't aware of the cause of their illness and don't report it to their doctors or local health officials. A recent study found that up to 1.5 million people get gastroenteritis at beaches in two counties in California each year. If this is the case, the number could be much higher.

Pathogens

Most illnesses that arise from contact with sewage are caused by pathogens, which are biological agents that cause disease or illness in a host. The most common pathogens in sewage are bacteria, parasites, and viruses. They cause a wide variety of acute illnesses including diarrhea and infections. These illnesses can be violent and unpleasant, but mostly pass after several days or weeks with no lasting effects. In some cases, however, pathogens can cause serious long-term illnesses or even death. Certain groups such as children, the elderly, and those with a weakened immune system are particularly vulnerable to these long-term effects. When the parasite *cryptosporidium* contaminated the drinking water supply in Milwaukee in 1993, 403,000 people became ill and 70–100 people died, the vast majority of whom had been HIV-positive. The illnesses caused by pathogens commonly found in untreated sewage are summarized below.

Bacteria	Acute Effects	Chronic or Ultimate Effects
E. coli 0157:H7	Diarrhea	Death, Hemolytic uremic syndrome
Legionella pneumoniae	Fever, pneumonia	Elderly: death
Helicobacter pylori	Gastritis	Ulcers and stomach cancer
Vibrio cholerae	Diarrhea	Death
Vibrio vulnificus	Skin and tissue infection	Death in those with liver problems
Campylobacter	Diarrhea	Death: Guillain-Barré syndrome
Salmonella	Diarrhea	Reactive arthritis

Bacteria	Acute Effects	Chronic or Ultimate Effects
Yersinia	Diarrhea	Reactive arthritis
Shigella	Diarrhea	Reactive arthritis
Cyanobacteria	Diarrhea	Potential cancer
Leptospirosis	Fever, headache, chills, muscle aches, vomiting	Weil's disease, kidney damage, liver failure, death
Aeromonas hydrophila	Diarrhea	
Parasites		
Giardia lamblia	Diarrhea	Children: Failure to develop physically and mentally
Cryptosporidium	Diarrhea	Immunocompromised: death
Toxoplasma Gondii	Newborn syndrome, hearing and visual loss, mental retardation	Dementia, seizures
Acanthamoeba	Eye infections	
Microsporidia	Diarrhea	
Entamoeba cayetanensis	Amebiasis, amoebic dysentery, abscess in liver or other organs	
Viruses		
Hepatitis viruses	Liver infection	Liver failure
Adenoviruses	Eye infections, diarrhea, respiratory disease	
Caliciviruses	Diarrhea	
Coxsackieviruses	Encephalitis, aseptic meningitis	Heart disease, diabetes
Echoviruses	Aseptic meningitis	
Polyomaviruses		Cancer of the colon

Toxic Algal Blooms

In addition to pathogens, the high nutrient levels in untreated sewage can cause illness when they create algal blooms. Algal blooms are rapid increases in the population of phytoplankton algae, or single-celled plants that serve as an important food source to other organisms. The nutrients in sewage act as fertilizers and cause the number of algae to swell. Some algae are toxic to humans who can come in contact with them from eating shellfish or swimming or boating in contaminated water. Symptoms from exposure include memory loss, vomiting, diarrhea, abdominal pain, liver failure, respiratory paralysis, and coma. If an affected person does not receive proper medical attention, some toxins can be fatal.

All people deserve clean water free of the many dangerous pollutants found in sewage.

Pharmaceuticals and Other Compounds

There is growing concern about the illnesses caused by pharmaceuticals, synthetic hormones, personal care products and other pollutants found in many waterways across the country. Many of them enter the environment through the sewage system. Certain compounds called endocrine disruptors may disrupt processes in humans that are controlled by hormones, including development, growth, and reproduction. These compounds are already thought to be causing cancer and genetic defects in fish. Little is known about how these chemicals affect human health over time and even less is known about how multiple chemicals interact in the human body. Contact with raw sewage could be having greater effects than we know.

Solutions Are Needed

All people deserve clean water free of the many dangerous pollutants found in sewage. The only way to ensure this is to stop sewage overflows and leaks and ensure that no sewage is released into the environment untreated. However, it would cost hundreds of billions of dollars and take decades to update the nation's wastewater infrastructure to this level. In recent years, funding for wastewater infrastructure has been cut instead. Until we make significant progress towards reducing the amount of sewage in our water, there must be strong notification programs that will allow people to know when there is a danger of contacting raw sewage. Wastewater facilities should be required to inform the media, citizens, and environmental agencies when they release untreated sewage into the environment. American Rivers works to pass legislation around the country to keep citizens informed of sewage contamination in their waterways. Not only will such programs allow people to stay healthy by avoiding raw sewage, but it will also build support for increasing funding for key infrastructure needs in the future.

3

Biosolids Are Safe

US Environmental Protection Agency

The US Environmental Protection Agency (EPA) is a federal bureau responsible for overseeing ecological standards in the United States.

Biosolids are treated sewage that in turn is used as fertilizer for agricultural products. The creation of biosolids provides an efficient way to prevent both environmental problems and the use of extensive landfill space for the disposal of sewage. Biosolids are heavily regulated by the EPA in order to assure safety and have been utilized in all fifty states to improve crop yield. Biosolids are also utilized in areas such as former mines (to help regenerate vegetation), in forestry, and in everyday composting. While biosolids are currently only being used on 1 percent of the agricultural land in the United States, they have already made a valuable contribution to American farming.

W*hat are Biosolids?*

They are nutrient-rich organic materials resulting from the treatment of domestic sewage in a treatment facility. When treated and processed, these residuals can be recycled and applied as fertilizer to improve and maintain productive soils and stimulate plant growth.

What is the difference between biosolids and sludge?

Biosolids are treated sewage sludge. Biosolids are carefully treated and monitored and must be used in accordance with regulatory requirements.

US Environmental Protection Agency, "Frequently Asked Questions," August 13, 2009. www.epa.gov.

Why do we have biosolids?

We have biosolids as a result of the wastewater treatment process. Water treatment technology has made our water safer for recreation and seafood harvesting. Thirty years ago, thousands of American cities dumped their raw sewage directly into the nation's rivers, lakes, and bays. Through regulation of this dumping, local governments are now required to treat wastewater and to make the decision whether to recycle biosolids as fertilizer, incinerate it, or bury it in a landfill.

Biosolids can be recycled and applied as fertilizer to improve and maintain productive soils and stimulate plant growth.

How are biosolids generated and processed?

Biosolids are created through the treatment of domestic wastewater generated from sewage treatment facilities. The treatment of biosolids can actually begin before the wastewater reaches the sewage treatment plant. In many larger wastewater treatment systems, pre-treatment regulations require that industrial facilities pre-treat their wastewater to remove many hazardous contaminants before it is sent to a wastewater treatment plant. Wastewater treatment facilities monitor incoming wastewater streams to ensure their recyclability and compatibility with the treatment plant process.

Once the wastewater reaches the plant, the sewage goes through physical, chemical and biological processes which clean the wastewater and remove the solids. If necessary, the solids are then treated with lime to raise the pH level to eliminate objectionable odors. The wastewater treatment processes sanitize wastewater solids to control pathogens (disease-causing organisms, such as certain bacteria, viruses and parasites) and other organisms capable of transporting disease.

How are biosolids used?

After treatment and processing biosolids can be recycled and applied as fertilizer to improve and maintain productive soils and stimulate plant growth. The controlled land application of biosolids completes a natural cycle in the environment. By treating sewage sludge, it becomes biosolids which can be used as valuable fertilizer, instead of taking up space in a landfill or other disposal facility.

Where are biosolids used?

Farmers and gardeners have been recycling biosolids for ages. Biosolids recycling is the process of beneficially using the treated residuals from wastewater treatment to promote the growth of agricultural crops, fertilize gardens and parks and reclaim mining sites. Land application of biosolids takes place in all 50 states.

Why are biosolids used on farms?

The application of biosolids reduces the need for chemical fertilizers. As more wastewater plants become capable of producing high quality biosolids, there is an even greater opportunity to make use of this valuable resource.

What percentage of biosolids are recycled and how many farms use biosolids?

About 50% of all biosolids are being recycled to land. These biosolids are used on less than one percent of the nation's agricultural land.

Are biosolids safe?

The National Academy of Sciences has reviewed current practices, public health concerns and regulator standards, and has concluded that "the use of these materials in the production of crops for human consumption when practiced in accordance with existing federal guidelines and regulations, presents negligible risk to the consumer, to crop production and to the environment."

Do biosolids smell?

Biosolids may have their own distinctive odor depending on the type of treatment they have been through. Some biosolids may have only a slight musty, ammonia odor. Others have a stronger odor that may be offensive to some people. Much of the odor is caused by compounds containing sulfur and ammonia, both of which are plant nutrients.

Are there regulations for the land application of biosolids?

The federal biosolids rule is contained in 40 CFR Part 503. Biosolids that are to be land applied must meet these strict regulations and quality standards. The Part 503 rule governing the use and disposal of biosolids contain numerical limits, for metals in biosolids, pathogen reduction standards, site restriction, crop harvesting restrictions and monitoring, record keeping and reporting requirements for land applied biosolids as well as similar requirements for biosolids that are surface disposed or incinerated. Most recently, standards have been proposed to include requirements in the Part 503 Rule that limit the concentration of dioxin and dioxin-like compounds in biosolids to ensure safe land application.

Where can I find out more about the regulations?

The biosolids rule is described in the EPA publication "A Plain English Guide to the EPA Part 503 Biosolids Rule." This guide states and interprets the Part 503 rule for the general reader. This guide is also available in hard copy. In addition to the "Plain English Guide," EPA has prepared "A Guide to the Biosolids Risk Assessments for the EPA Part 503 Rule," which shows the many steps followed to develop the scientifically defensible, safe set of rules (also available from EPA in hard copy.)

How are biosolids used for agriculture?

Biosolids are used to fertilize fields for raising crops. Agricultural use of biosolids, that meet strict quality criteria and application rates, have been shown to produce significant improvements in crop growth and yield. Nutrients found in biosolids, such as nitrogen, phosphorus and potassium and trace elements such as calcium, copper, iron, magnesium, manganese, sulfur and zinc, are necessary for crop production and growth. The use of biosolids reduces the farmer's production costs and replenishes the organic matter that has been depleted over time. The organic matter improves soil structure by increasing the soil's ability to absorb and store moisture.

The organic nitrogen and phosphorous found in biosolids are used very efficiently by crops because these plant nutrients are released slowly throughout the growing season. This enables the crop to absorb these nutrients as the crop grows. This efficiency lessens the likelihood of groundwater pollution by nitrogen and phosphorous.

Biosolids may be composted and sold or distributed for use on lawns and home gardens.

Can biosolids be used for mine reclamation?

Biosolids have been used successfully at mine sites to establish sustainable vegetation. Not only does the organic matter, inorganic matrix and nutrients present in the biosolids reduce the bioavailability of toxic substances often found in highly disturbed mine soils, but also regenerate the soil layer. This regeneration is very important for reclaiming abandoned mine sites with little or no topsoil. The biosolids application rate for mine reclamation is generally higher than the agronomic rate which cannot be exceeded for use of agricultural soils.

How are biosolids used for forestry?

Biosolids have been found to promote rapid timber growth, allowing quicker and more efficient harvest of an important natural resource.

Can biosolids be used for composting?

Yes, biosolids may be composted and sold or distributed for use on lawns and home gardens. Most biosolids composts are highly desirable products that are easy to store, transport and use. . . .

Can anyone apply biosolids to land?

Anyone who wants to use biosolids for land application must comply with all relevant federal and state regulations. In some cases a permit may be required.

What will it mean for a wastewater treatment plant, biosolids manager or land applier to agree to follow an Environmental Management System (EMS) for Biosolids?

A voluntary EMS is now being developed for biosolids by the National Biosolids Partnership (NBP). The NBP consists of members from the Association of Metropolitan Sewerage Agency, the Water Environment Federation, the U.S. Environmental Protection Agency (EPA) and other stakeholders, including the general public. Those facilities who pledge to follow the EMS are agreeing to follow community-friendly practices in addition to being in compliance with applicable state and Federal regulations. Community friendly practices refer to the control of odor, traffic, noise, and dust as well as the management of nutrients.

4

Biosolids Are Unsafe

Josh Harkinson

Josh Harkinson is a reporter for Mother Jones, *a bimonthly independent newsmagazine published by the Foundation for National Progress.*

Since 1987, the US Environmental Protection Agency (EPA) has been promoting the use of biosolids. Biosolids are treated sewage that is being used throughout the United States for everything from agriculture products to lawn care. Unfortunately, the EPA has either ignored or shown little concern for many of the problems that are being caused by biosolids. One problem is that sewage also frequently includes medical and industrial waste; as with other fertilizers and pesticides, these chemicals can potentially contaminate water supplies and air quality. A number of people have publically questioned the EPA's regulation of biosolids, but the agency has been slow to respond to criticism. While biosolids may be one method for dealing with sewage, there remain too many unknowns. Instead, there is a need to find other, safer methods for converting sewage into usable products.

In August 1987, the National Park Service tore up the White House's South Lawn and tilled in heaps of a new, locally produced fertilizer. The weedy plot's transformation into a carpet of green caught gardeners' attention, and soon there was a waiting list to buy bags of ComPro, a compost made from nearby wastewater plants' solid effluent, a.k.a. sewage sludge. Four years later, dumping sewage into the ocean was banned, and sludge went national. The Environmental Protection Agency launched a PR [public relations] push to rebrand it as an all-purpose soil conditioner and fertilizer it innocuously called "biosolids." If sludge was good enough for the first family, the agency reminded us, then surely it was good enough for the rest of America. "The Clintons are walking around on poo," the EPA's sludge chief quipped in 1998. "But it's very clean poo."

Today, more than half the 15 trillion gallons of sewage Americans flush annually is biologically scrubbed, "dewatered," and processed into products with names like BioEdge, Nitrohumus, and Vital Cycle and spread on farmland, lawns, and home vegetable gardens. (The rest is incinerated or landfilled.) Recycling sewage is big business: In 2007 the Carlyle Group paid $772 million for the sludge-residuals company Synagro, whose products are the most popular on the market. Sludge could be the ultimate growth industry; as one trade publication observes dryly, "There will continue to be more wastewater solids to manage with every passing year."

In theory, recycling poop is the perfect solution to the one truly unavoidable byproduct of human civilization. Turning sewage into a potent, inexpensive fertilizer means cleaner rivers and oceans. But as sludge has spread across the country, so have concerns that it may cause as many environmental problems as it solves. In communities where sludge has been used, residents have reported ailments ranging from migraines to pneumonia to mysterious deaths. In a 1994 episode often cited by sludge foes, an 11-year-old Pennsylvania boy died of a staph infection after biking through sludge at an abandoned mine.

Sludge's Dirty Secret

Sludge's dirty secret is that it may contain anything that goes down the drain—from Prozac flushed down toilets to motor oil hosed from factory floors. While sludge sold to consumers must be virtually pathogen free, sludge used on farms and industrial sites is permitted to contain low levels of human pathogens. A federal radiation task force recently warned that sludge might be contaminated with radioactive waste; in January, shipments of Canadian sludge with elevated radioactivity levels were turned back at the border. Food companies such as Del Monte and H.J. Heinz won't accept produce grown on sludge-treated land. The Netherlands and Switzerland effectively ban the use of sludge on farmland, and 37 states regulate it more strictly than the EPA.

Despite the growing stink, the EPA has remained bullish on sludge through three presidential administrations. It points out that sludge has never been conclusively linked to any serious illnesses or deaths. Critics say the agency has consistently ignored the risks. "The fight over sludge is not about sewage; it's about hiding industrial waste," says Ed Hallman, an attorney for a former EPA scientist who has accused the agency of covering up the dangers of sludge. "The chemicals absorbed in sludge don't exist anymore as far as the EPA is concerned. They are gone."

Some scientists are concerned that dangerous levels of contaminants from sludge are passing into crops and groundwater as well as blowing off fields and becoming airborne.

Complaints about sludge usually begin with the smell. One morning last August [2008], a manure spreader spewed a brown pudding on a field behind Barry Kimbrough's house in Lawrence County, Alabama. "It smelled exactly like what it is—it smelled like shit," recalls Kimbrough, a retiree with a small cattle ranch. "The odor was so bad, some people had to move out of their house for a week or so." Other neighbors complained of breathing problems or pneumonia.

The EPA acknowledges that "biosolids may have their own distinctive odor," but it doesn't regulate their smell. Multiple studies have shown that severe odors can cause health problems, including depression and stress that can lead to chronic hypertension and heart disease. Jimmy Slaughter, a lawyer for Synagro, notes that smelling sludge can elicit "a visceral reaction." Yet, he says, "If we were causing health problems, we would have known [it] a long time ago."

But the stench is just the start. A recent EPA survey of sludge samples from across the US found nearly universal contamination by 10 flame retardants and 12 pharmaceuticals and exceptionally high levels of endocrine disruptors such as triclosan, an ingredient in antibacterial soap that scientists believe is killing amphibians.

Toxic Waste

The EPA, however, hasn't assessed the safety of many of these chemicals. (The Government Accountability Office recently concluded that the agency's toxics program is "at serious risk of becoming obsolete.") Though it limits the amount of toxic substances that can be dumped into the sewers, with the exception of several heavy metals such as cadmium and lead, the EPA doesn't test for contaminants when they come out the other end of the pipes, where they may be concentrated in sludge. Some scientists are concerned that dangerous levels of contaminants from sludge are passing into crops and groundwater as well as blowing off fields and becoming airborne. Studies have shown that some chemicals in sludge can interact with one another to become more persistent or toxic. Other research has suggested that the toxins in sludge can pass into milk and meat.

In 1979, a Georgia dairyman named Andy McElmurray started applying locally produced sludge fertilizer to his fields. Over the next several years, nearly half his 700 cows died from severe diarrhea. The EPA didn't test his soil, but McElmurray hired his own experts, who concluded that his sludge had contained high levels of thallium. A toxic metal that is the active ingredient in rat poison, thallium rarely turns up in sewage, but it was used as a catalyst by a nearby NutraSweet factory. When McElmurray's experts sampled a local milk brand, they detected thallium at levels more than 11 times above the legal limit for drinking water.

McElmurray sued the federal government for disaster relief, claiming sludge had destroyed his farm. He finally won the case last year [2008]. "I believe that if the farmer knew the truth, he would never put sludge on his farmland," he says. "It's all a smoke-and-mirrors game that the EPA has played." His view was echoed by the federal judge who ruled in his favor, finding that "senior EPA officials took extraordinary steps to quash scientific dissent and any questioning of the EPA's biosolids program."

Whistleblowers inside the agency have made similar claims. Last year, Hugh Kaufman, a former EPA investigator, testified in a lawsuit that former administrator Christine Todd Whitman prevented him from looking into the agency's biosolids program. More than a decade earlier, David Lewis, a senior researcher at the EPA's lab in Athens, Georgia, publicly criticized the agency for not doing enough research on sludge. In response, the EPA accused him of unlawfully engaging in a partisan debate. (The Labor Department overturned the complaint.) After Lewis continued to publish alarming studies about sludge in *Nature* and other journals, the EPA scientist in charge of promoting biosolids gave a sludge-company lawyer a Synagro document that said Lewis had been conducting "uninformed, unsupported, and otherwise unsound science." (Lewis, who retired in 2003 and has since sued the EPA, declined to comment for this article.)

In 2002, the National Academy of Sciences joined the calls for more research. The EPA launched an ongoing round of studies in partnership with the Water Environment Research

Foundation [WERF], the nonprofit research arm of the sewage industry's main lobbying organization. In 2006, WERF funded Steve Wing, an epidemiology professor at the University of North Carolina, to develop a standardized way to track illnesses reported near sludge sites—something most experts agree is urgently needed. Wing says WERF pressured him "to keep the industry's interest in mind" by micromanaging his work.

WERF "definitely can't be trusted as an honest broker," says John Stauber, coauthor of *Toxic Sludge Is Good for You!*, which exposed the hyping of sludge. "It's like trusting the nuclear industry to be an honest broker when disposing of nuclear waste." Dan Woltering, WERF'S head of research, denies that the group meddled with Wing's research. WERF, he asserts, does "sound, peer-reviewed research" and does not have a policy agenda.

Regulation Is Lacking

The official response to new discoveries of contaminated sludge remains tepid. In May 2007, the EPA learned that sludge had contaminated as many as 5,000 acres of grazing land about 25 miles from Kimbrough's Alabama ranch with perfluorooctanoic acid (PFOA), a probable carcinogen used in Teflon. The chemical was traced back to a local manufacturer that had dumped contaminated wastewater straight into the sewer. The case prompted the EPA to issue its first-ever advisory on PFOA in drinking water, but it did not ban the dumping of the chemical into sewers or require sludge to be tested for it. Even though the exceedingly high PFOA concentrations in the Lawrence County fields could pose a health threat to animals or humans, as of press time, the Department of Agriculture hadn't tested local cattle for the chemical.

Why does the EPA remain so unconcerned about sludge? Much of it is expediency, maintains Stauber. "You had some individuals who decided that 'out of sight, out of mind' would be the easiest way to handle this massive toxic disposal problem," he says.

Suzanne Rudzinski, who oversees bio-solids in the EPA's Office of Water, says the agency's approach has been prudent and balanced. "There's always somebody, no matter who, that doesn't like what the EPA is doing," she says. She grants that the pervasiveness of flame retardants and other chemicals in sludge is a concern, but would like to see more research before recommending whether to regulate them. "I think we agree that there's a lot more that we could learn," she says, "and that's what we're trying to do."

But Chris Nidel, the attorney for two Virginia families that recently resolved a lawsuit with Synagro, says the EPA's wait-and-see stance is nothing but wishful thinking: "This is an experiment—with the initial results being negative—that we are going to continue ad nauseam until we have a regulatory agency that has a backbone."

Leftover sludge is often incinerated, releasing heavy metals into the air and packing landfills with enough ash each year to fill more than 3,100 dump trucks.

Disposing of Sludge

Might there be a better way to get rid of sludge? Perhaps, thanks to this nifty fact: A single American's daily sludge output can generate enough power to light a 60-watt bulb for more than nine hours a day. Sludge is rich in methane, the main component of natural gas. That means that the wastewater sector, which uses about 1 percent of the nation's electricity, could power itself with sludge and possibly have wattage to spare.

So far, however, fewer than 10 percent of the nation's 6,000 public wastewater plants have anaerobic digesters that can extract methane from sludge; of those, just 20 percent burn the gas for energy. However, other promising projects are under way. Flint, Michigan, is one of several cities worldwide to fuel buses with gas from sludge. Last summer, Los Angeles began injecting sludge into a mile-deep well, where pressure and heat are expected to release enough methane to power 1,000 homes.

Sludge power is only a partial solution. At best, methane removal cuts sludge's volume in half. Currently, leftover sludge is often incinerated, releasing heavy metals into the air and packing landfills with enough ash each year to fill more than 3,100 dump trucks. New high-efficiency poop-to-power plants can minimize those impacts. Using high-temperature or low-oxygen reactions, they covert sludge into a synthetic gas or oil, or a char similar to barbecue briquettes. The process can produce twice as much energy as it consumes, says Brian Dooley, a spokesman for Atlanta-based EnerTech, which built the first commercial plant of its kind in Southern California last year. The plant converts sludge from about a third of Los Angeles and Orange counties into a char that replaces coal at a local cement kiln; its ash is mixed into the cement. Such efforts, which reduce landfilling and emissions, have earned praise from some anti-sludge groups. Caroline Snyder, the founder of Citizens for Sludge-Free Land, calls it a "win-win situation."

The EPA says sludge power holds promise, but it's not quite ready to quit pushing sludge as a wonder fertilizer. This hasn't deterred the sewage industry, which sees a chance to get into the renewable energy business and put a stop to the stream of health complaints and costly lawsuits. "After almost 40 years of working in bio-solids," a WERF official wrote in a recent newsletter, "I never thought I'd say this: it is an exciting time for sludge!"

5

Humanure Can Make Sewage More Manageable

Catherine Price

Catherine Price is a contributing editor to Popular Science *magazine.*

While most Americans accept sewage systems that safely contain human waste as the norm, these systems are fairly new in history. In the past, most human waste was used to fertilize crops. Today, there is a small but growing movement of people who wish to return to a more basic treatment of human waste. Instead of using traditional toilets and the public wastewater system, individuals are using composting toilets, allowing them to create—over a period of time—humanure. This product is then used in the same way that other composting material is used: as soil or plant nutrients. Unlike biosolids, chemicals are not added to humanure. While proponents believe that composting toilets offer a better way to treat human waste, their vision may be more difficult to sell to the average American. Unlike the typical flush toilet, composting toilets require more effort at upkeep and maintenance. Nonetheless, composting toilets offer an environmentally healthy alternative to traditional toilets and a workable solution for the 2.6 billion people around the world who have no toilets at all.

Laura Allen, a 33-year-old teacher from Oakland, California, has a famous toilet. To be honest, it's actually a box, covered in decorative ceramic tiles, sitting on the cement floor of her bathroom like a throne. No pipes lead to or from it; instead, a bucket full of shavings from a local wood shop rests on the box next to the seat with a note instructing users to add a scoopful after making their "deposit." Essentially an indoor outhouse, it's a composting toilet, a sewerless system that Allen uses to collect her household's excrement and transform it into a rich brown material known to fans as "humanure."

Allen is a founding member of an activist group devoted to the end of sewage as we know it. Her toilet recently made an appearance in the *Los Angeles Times*—which might explain why she didn't seem surprised when I emailed her out of the blue to ask if I could use it.

The crazy thing isn't the idea of using our crap as fertilizer. It's how far we've strayed.

Lifting the seat, she showed me a seal of insulating foam tape she'd put around its edges to prevent odors from wafting into the bathroom and then pointed out a funnel-like contraption hanging from the front of the toilet that diverted urine away from crap. The separated waste collected in two containers sitting several feet below the toilet seat, accessible through a hatch cut into the side of the house: the urine flowed into a plastic jug formerly used for olive oil, the feces into a bucket labeled "feta cheese." A year from now, once it's composted, Allen and her roommates will use this excrement to fertilize their fruit trees.

To most Americans, Allen's system would seem eccentric, if not downright weird. But while feta cheese buckets are relatively new creations, humans have used shit as fertilizer since the dawn of agriculture—the nitrogen in our urine is an excellent fertilizer, and feces, itself nutrient-rich, is a great soil amendment. It wasn't until the turn of the 20th century that water-based sewer systems became commonplace in the United States; after that, "sewer farms," where crops were irrigated with untreated wastewater, were commonplace. Even today, the majority of the world's population doesn't have access to flush toilets, making us the anomaly, rather than the norm.

As public health advocates will be quick to point out, the switch to sewers helps protect us from sewage borne diseases. But it also breaks the nutrient cycle: instead of returning nutrients to the land from where they came, we now reclassify excrement as waste and use chemical fertilizers to replace it. From an agricultural standpoint, the crazy thing isn't the idea of using our crap as fertilizer. It's how far we've strayed.

Humanure and Biosolids

With this in mind, the idea behind our current system would seem to make sense: more than half of America's sewage sludge is applied to land. But there's a crucial difference between humanure and modern sludge, known in the sewage industry as "biosolids." Humanure is made from pure human excrement. It can still contain residues from pharmaceuticals that pass through our bodies, but it lacks the industrial chemicals or other contaminants that make sludge so controversial.

Biosolids, on the other hand, can count as ingredients everything that's dumped into our sewer system, including a mixture of domestic and industrial waste that can include heavy metals, toxic chemicals, and thousands of other pollutants—and its long-term effects on soil are impossible to predict. The main ingredient of biosolids and humanure— feces—might be the same, but when it comes to their potential to contaminate soil, the two materials are fundamentally different.

It's difficult to judge what will ultimately have worse consequences for agriculture and human health: spreading the contaminants in modern sewage sludge on soil or diverting sewage's nutrients away from land. (Both are bad in different ways.) But one thing is certain: creating pure humanure with our current wastewater treatment system would require segregating our waste streams at their sources, which, thanks to the way our sewers are piped, is impossible to do.

Allen left me alone so that I could experience her bathroom firsthand and then took me outside to see the next step in the process. We walked through a small chicken coop to three 55-gallon barrels full of decomposing feces arranged in a row next to the side of the house, each of which would sit for at least a year in order to compost thoroughly. Covered with netting to prevent flies and plastic lids to keep out rain, they didn't smell.

A small but growing number of Americans is unhooking from septic tanks and sewer systems (or, in some cases, never hooking up) and composting their waste.

But then Allen reached for a compost auger—a corkscrew-like device with a hand crank that breaks apart the composting material and adds oxygen—and worked it into the compost. The air filled with the strong, unpleasant odor of methane, a byproduct of anaerobic composting.

"It must have gotten some water into it, that's why it smells so bad," Allen said, pulling up the auger and revealing some confused-looking earthworms. She examined the moist brown material clinging to the corkscrew. "This one's probably about seven months old."

The Humanure Movement

Allen and her roommates' devotion to their toilet is unusual, but they're far from alone—a small but growing number of Americans is unhooking from septic tanks and sewer systems (or, in some cases, never hooking in) and composting their waste. If you want to get a sense of how excited people can get about the results, check out the website of a man named Joseph Jenkins. A slate-roofing contractor in Pennsylvania who's been shitting in a bucket since the 1970s, Jenkins and his followers dream of a day where entire cities might compost their excrement, with municipal collection services similar to today's recycling programs.

To help jumpstart the revolution, Jenkins self-published a guide in 2005 called *The Humanure Handbook* that features chapters with titles like "Crap Happens" and an illustrated character named "Tommy the Turd." For his first run, Jenkins could only afford to print 600 copies; he's now sold more than 33,000, and portions of the handbook have been translated into Spanish, Norweigan, Korean, Hebrew, Mongolian and Chinese.

The challenge these simple systems face, however, is that most Americans don't like the idea of homemade toilets. We don't like thinking about our shit, period. So a middle ground has emerged; commercially designed toilets that look like what you're used to, but have composting systems built in.

Successful composting, while not rocket science, requires attention, devotion and considerable knowledge of the process.

The BioLet, originally a Swedish design, includes a heater to speed decomposition and aerates its contents with mechanized arms. The Sun-Mar has a built-in crank and a removable tray that catches finished material. The Envirolet, the American version of a design by a Norweigan company called Vera Miljö, uses a carousel system—sort of like a lazy Susan—to keep batches separate so that new waste doesn't mix with old. Biolytix, an Australian wastewater treatment system designed to fit into a conventional septic tank, comes pre-seeded with an ecosystem of worms, beetles and microorganisms that filter and break down waste.

Bio-Sun, Aquatron, Equaris, Phoenix—like "biosolids," they all manage to sound vaguely green while avoiding any allusions to the substance they're meant to treat. Talk to people who have owned them, though, and there's no getting around that what you're dealing with is shit. With a typical toilet, all you need to do is flush; with a composting toilet, everything you produce stays right where you left it—and some of these commercial designs, while tempting, aren't big enough to handle daily use. (Horror stories abound.)

Composting Toilets

Successful composting, while not rocket science, requires attention, devotion and considerable knowledge of the process; far from being an informational brochure, *The Humanure Handbook*, is 255 pages long. The environmentalist in me wanted to embrace the idea behind Allen's toilet—really, I did—but when it came to dealing with my own excrement, I was like most Americans; the only time I wanted to look back in the bathroom was to flush.

To find out if there were any way to create a composting toilet that wouldn't make an average American recoil in disgust, I traveled to Bainbridge Island, a 35-minute ferry ride from Seattle. My destination was IslandWood, an outdoor learning center tucked into 255 wooded acres of a former tree farm that's home to one of the country's only large-scale composting toilets. Known as the Clivus Multrum M-15, this particular system can handle up to 36,000 uses per year.

When I reached IslandWood, I was welcomed by Brian Bonifaci, the man responsible for maintaining the Clivus system. Dressed in Carhartt clothing from top to bottom, Bonifaci led me to the basement room where the compost was collected in two large, gray boxes. With sloping floors designed to make it easier to remove finished material, each bin was nearly 10 feet long and over seven feet high, with thick black pipes connecting them to four toilets sitting directly above.

After showing me a trap door where finished compost could be removed, Bonifaci opened a hatch on the upper part of the box so that I could see what was inside: a giant mound of feces, toilet paper, and wood chips. It was level except for an upside down cone that had formed where the most recent deposits had dropped. But even though my face was practically in the box, I couldn't smell its contents—an exhaust fan was constantly pulling fresh air into the bin and out a vent on the roof so that no odors could leak into the room where I was standing. (The same fan also pulled air down the toilet so the smell couldn't escape upwards into the bathroom.)

"What do you need to do to maintain this?" I asked Bonifaci.

"I add a bucket of wood chips once a week and rake down the cone when it gets too high," he said. "That's about it."

He explained that the fan helped aerate the pile, eliminating the need to turn the compost, and an automatic moistening system added just enough water to keep the material from getting too dry. Eventually, Bonifaci told me, they'd have to remove some of the compost from the bottom of the pile, but so far they hadn't had to, despite the fact that they'd installed the toilet in 2002—composting dramatically reduces the volume of waste.

But then again, IslandWood's facilities weren't exactly getting their maximum 36,000 uses per year—Bonifaci told me that some campers, fearful about the toilets' gaping black holes, simply held it till they got to a different building. So I called Don Mills, the sales director for Clivus Multrum, to find out more about what these systems' capacities really were.

A Difficult Market

Mills, who refuses to use the word "biosolid" unless he can add in a "so-called" before it, has strong opinions on the current way America deals with sewage.

"I'm calling that shit 'sludge' until I die," he announced when I used the word "biosolids" without his preferred modifier. "And I might die from it!"

He then launched into a tirade against land application. But when the subject switched to composting toilets, Mills became cautiously optimistic.

"Look," he said. "Selling composting toilets is an uphill struggle, partially because of the psychology around shit and also because of regulations."

But once you sell people on the idea, said Mills, "there's no capacity limitation with this technology. We can build it for as many people as would need to use any toilet, any place." If a bathroom is meant to serve more people than a single Clivus Multrum system can handle, you just add more bins or toilets. Clivus Multrum has a system installed at the Bronx Zoo, for example, that's designed for over 500,000 uses a year.

Mills explained that there are ways to make composting toilets less offensive—Clivus Multrum already has models that use a small amount of foam to "flush" the excrement to a hidden holding tank, which means the toilets don't have to sit directly over the composting bins and users don't have to look down onto a giant mound of shit. Less hands-on customers than Bonifaci can also contract Clivus Multrum to maintain the toilets for them.

The best solution for the future, it seems, just might be a modernized version of the past.

"If this were something that were supported by the government," Mills said, "if the compost toilet was made a requirement, then many things would change." Toilets would be designed to be even more palatable to non-environmentalists, he said, and large-scale municipal collection systems would evolve to get the compost out of the toilets and onto fields.

Mill is not entirely optimistic—like me, he doubts that composting toilets will become mainstream in America any time soon. Manhattan's skyscrapers weren't built with humanure in mind, and as he himself admits, "the dry toilet at IslandWood is not something most homeowners would regard as satisfactory in their dream house."

The Future of Composting

But there are plenty of places in the world not yet hooked up to sewer systems—in fact, an estimated 2.6 billion people don't even have access to toilets. Just as many developing countries adopted cell phones without ever having built the infrastructure for landline phones, poor communities could skip sewer systems and develop an integrated system of composting toilets instead.

In India, where 18 percent of the population lacks toilets, a man named Dr. Bindeshwar Pathak, founder of the Sulabh Sanitation Movement, is helping people do just that: he's developed a line of composting toilets that earned him the prestigious 2009 Stockholm Water Prize. According to the Stockholm Water Institute, the Sulabh Shauchalaya twin pit, pour-flush toilet is being used in more than 1.2 million residences and buildings in India, and its public facilities—spread across 7500 locations—are getting more than 10 million uses per day.

America's a tougher market. But if composting toilets were inoffensive to use, if someone else were responsible for dealing with the compost—just as right now someone else is responsible for treating our watered-down waste—it's possible to imagine new buildings and communities that incorporate at least some of the recycling schemes of which the humanurists dream. We probably will never eliminate American sludge entirely, but if we were able to divert even a small portion of our excrement away from the sewer system, treat it for pathogens and turn it into compost, we'd be reducing the amount left to deal with. The best solution for the future, it seems, just might be a modernized version of the past.

Back at IslandWood, I asked Bonifaci if I could try out the facilities, and soon found myself alone in the restroom. Thanks to the fan sucking air into the toilet, the only noticeable odor was a faint aura of lemongrass cleaning products and the lingering scent of lavender soap. Since the Clivus Multrum doesn't divert urine, when I sat down, I didn't have to aim. The biggest tangible difference between it and a conventional toilet was the breeze—which, if you're not expecting it, can be a little surprising. But there was no odor, no wood chips, no worry that in a week or two or three, I'd be responsible for handling the waste I'd just produced.

The experience was remarkably unremarkable. It required so little thought that when I got up, I didn't even need to turn back to flush.

6

Sewage Should Be Regulated and Used to Irrigate Crops Around the World

Fred Pearce

Fred Pearce is the author of When Rivers Run Dry *and* Turning Up the Heat.

In much of the world, it remains common to use raw sewage to irrigate crops. While many farmers attest that raw sewage accelerates the growth of agricultural produce, the health effects remain unknown. Using sewage to increase farming yields may make sense, especially when the disposal of sewage in a growing world population creates multiple problems, but only if the sewage is treated at facilities that remove pathogens that may be dangerous to people.

I advise against eating vegetables bought in the markets of Vadodara, a large industrial city in southern Gujarat in India. Most likely they will have been irrigated with neat industrial effluent [outflow from a sewer system or other liquid waste] from the town's numerous chemical plants. The effluent pours down a drain that runs for 40 miles from the city's industrial zone to the sea. The drain is a river that "never runs dry," one farmer told me. "You can get as much water as you want, when you want it. It's an assured supply of water, unlike the wells here." (The wells, I need hardly mention, run dry because the chemical companies are emptying underground water reserves.)

The drain is not something you would want to go near. I peered beneath one of its concrete covers, which have everywhere been broken by farmers trying to get at the liquid. There was a tarry scum on the surface. It was jet black, though I was told that at different times it took different colors, depending on the effluent of the day. The stench was sometimes unbearable—a mixture of solvents and paints and much else that I couldn't recognize. But all along the road beside the drain, for dozens of miles, there were plastic pipes trained across the potholed surface, siphoning the toxic treacle onto fields and into villages. Legally, pumping from the drain was banned. But "during droughts especially, some of the officials of the company running the canal turn a blind eye," said my guide, a local investigator called Vaibhav Bhamoriva.

Across the poor, developing world, raw sewage is increasingly being used for irrigating crops.

Dozens of firms, from the giant Hindustan Petrochemical Corporation to backyard outfits like the Shree Bitumen Company, dump their waste into the drain. Some 20 million gallons flow down it to the sea each day. And, said Bhamoriva, tens of thousands of people in more than forty villages rely on it to grow their crops. It is the basis for a vibrant local economy. After interviewing hundreds of farmers, he has calculated that the total output of crops from effluent-irrigated fields here is worth half a million dollars a year. Some farmers use the effluent to grow rice; more grow sugarcane or millet. Most frighteningly, a lot grow fruit and vegetables, which are sold in the city market. "The sellers mix the vegetables grown from effluent with all the other fruit and vegetables. So we all eat it," one farmer told me. "We farmers know about it, but in the town nobody knows what they are eating."

Farming with Dirty Water

What is the health effect of all this? In truth, nobody knows. Officially, the farmers are not allowed to use the effluent, so officially there is no problem. I dropped in at Chokari, a village of 1500 people living on either side of the toxic canal. The villagers told me that they had no other source of water except a pump more than half a mile away that they use for drinking. The contents of the drain were used to irrigate fields of rice, millet, and vegetables. Farming with the stuff was not pleasant work. "Sometimes the smell when we are watering our fields is unbearable," one told me. "We avoid getting the liquid on our bodies, because sometimes it burns the skin. We watch the water, and if it changes color, sometimes we stop irrigating." They knew nothing about any longer-term effects on their bodies. But they said that it killed their soils. After three or four years, the chemicals destroyed the soil's fertility, leaving behind a cake of salt. They had to abandon the fields then. Eventually there would be no fields left, and perhaps no healthy farmers. But for now they made a living.

By a perverse irony, the drain in places runs less than a hundred yards from a canal built to carry clean water from the newly dammed Narmada River in the south of the state. But while the drain runs black and full, the canal has sat empty for some years. I spoke to one farmer who lost most of his land twenty years before to make way for the canal. He was resigned to the black humor of his situation. "Last year, during the election campaign, they released some water down the canal," he said. "But we've had none since." The toxic effluent, however, was always available.

Water should be recycled. Most of us would instinctively agree with that—until, perhaps, we realize what that means sometimes. Should dirty water be recycled? Nobody should countenance using neat industrial effluent to water crops. But sewage may be another matter. After all, even in Europe the concentrated muck created at sewage treatment plants is sometimes packaged up and sold as fertilizer for farmers. And in high-tech Singapore, officials announced plans in 2003 to add volume to the city-state's main drinking-water reservoir by topping it up with a 2.5 percent dose of recycled sewage effluent. That is small potatoes compared with London, whose inhabitants drink water that has been drunk and excreted several times as it makes its way down the Thames, being extracted and returned by towns such as Swindon, Reading, and Maidenhead before it reaches the capital. The advanced water-treatment technologies in use at every step make it as safe as water anywhere, despite its unappetizing recent history. The water-treatment plants have become just another loop in the water cycle.

In Pakistan, sewage irrigates a quarter of the country's vegetables.

Irrigating with Sewage

But across the poor, developing world, raw sewage is increasingly being used for irrigating crops. Chris Scott, of the International Water Management Institute, has conducted the first global survey of the practice. He has come to the staggering conclusion that perhaps a tenth of all the world's irrigated crops—everything from rice and wheat to lettuces, tomatoes, mangoes, and coconuts—are watered by the smelly, lumpy stuff coming out of the end of sewer pipes that empty the drains of big cities. Without it, much of the world would go hungry. In many countries—India, China, and Pakistan, to name just three of the biggest—there is very little sewage treatment, and yet a great deal of the sewage ends up being poured onto fields anyway, complete with disease-causing pathogens and sometimes laced with toxic waste from industry.

Scott estimates that more than 50 million acres of the world's farms are irrigated with sewage. And business is booming. The practice is most frequent on the fringes of the developing world's great cities, where clean water can be in desperately short supply in the dry season while sewer pipes keep gushing their contents onto the nearest open land all year round. In Hyderabad, the Indian city where he works, "pretty much 100 percent of the crops grown around the city rely on sewage. There is no other water available."

And however much consumers may squirm, farmers like it that way—first because the sewage is rich in nitrates and phosphates that fertilize their crops free of charge, and second because the supply is often much more reliable than clean water from rivers or irrigation canals, which means farmers can grow high-value crops that need constant watering, such as vegetables.

For these reasons, farms hooked up to sewage pipes make bigger profits than their rivals who rely on clean irrigation water. In Pakistan, farmers using sewage for irrigation typically earn $300 to $600 more annually than those without the benefit of sewage, says Scott. In West Africa, he met one farmer who grew twelve crops of lettuce a year on his sewage farm. You can see the benefits in land prices as well. In parts of Pakistan, it costs twice as much to buy fields watered by sewage pipes as neighboring fields irrigated with clean water. People downstream like the farmers, too. They are essentially operating a free municipal wastewater treatment service that stops rivers and reservoirs from stinking so much. And so, often secretly, do governments. The system feeds the people. In Pakistan, sewage irrigates a quarter of the country's vegetables.

The Dangers of Sewage

Many would say that the risks outweigh the benefits. Those risks include disease among farmers and customers and environmental problems such as the buildup of heavy metals and

unwanted nutrients in the soil and underground water reserves. "Right now," says Scott, "wastewater irrigation is in an
institutional no man's land. Water, health, and agriculture
ministries in many countries ban the practice but refuse to
recognize that it is widespread." But, he says, instead of trying
to outlaw it or pretending that it does not exist, governments
ought to regulate it. "We need to recognize that sewage is a
valuable resource that grows huge amounts of food. So instead we should help the millions of farmers involved to do it
better."

That means keeping sewage effluent for irrigating nonfood
crops or crops that will be processed or cooked before being
eaten. Obviously, it is more dangerous to pour sewage onto a
field of lettuce than a field of cotton, or even sugarcane. And
ultimately it means working toward treatment to make sewage
safe. In a handful of countries—most notably Israel, Jordan,
Tunisia, and Mexico—that is already happening. Sewage is
treated to remove pathogens before being released to farmers.
In these countries, recycling forms part of a national strategy
for maximizing water use and making sure valuable nutrients
are not wasted.

Mexico recycles enough treated wastewater to irrigate
around 600,000 acres. I visited a giant new state-of-the-art
sewage treatment plant at Juarez, El Paso's twin city on the
Rio Grande, which treats half the city's sewage and delivers
enough effluent down a canal to irrigate 75,000 acres. It is virtually the only source of water for crops downstream on the
Mexican side of the river. Israel converts around 70 percent of
the wastewater from its cities into treated effluent for irrigating export crops such as tomatoes and oranges. This is an effective addition to its national water supply of about a fifth.

This makes good sense. In urban areas, almost every drop
of water brought to the city to fill faucets eventually leaves
again as sewage effluent or in industrial waste. Where it can
be made safe, it should not be wasted.

7

Biofuel Can Turn Sewage Wastewater into a Power Resource

Greg Breining

Greg Breining writes about travel, science, and nature for a variety of publications, including National Geographic *and* Audubon.

In Minnesota and many other places, scientists have begun to focus on making biofuel from algae grown in treated sewage wastewater. The process has several advantages over other biofuel methods: crop yields are more efficient than soybeans, for instance, and the cost of the treated sewage is minimal. Even the National Aeronautics and Space Administration has considered using biofuel for its rockets. While the process for creating biofuels from treated sewage wastewater is promising, much more work will be required to refine the process. In particular, the current method used for extracting fuel from the algae is too expensive to make biofuels from sewage affordable.

In his quest for a fuel of the future, Roger Ruan has found a valuable resource in something nobody else wants—the wastewater from Minneapolis' largest sewage treatment plant.

The University of Minnesota professor is tapping into this rather unlikely source to grow single-celled algae and produce a diesel-like biofuel. He is one of many researchers around the world working to make biofuel from algae at a price that is competitive with gasoline and diesel fuel. But Ruan's project— along with several other sewage-to-fuel experiments—has a distinct advantage over competing algae-to-fuel efforts: His nutrient-rich feedstock is free and available at a nearly constant rate all year long.

A single acre of algae, even in an inefficient open pond, can produce 5,000 gallons of biodiesel per year.

And perhaps most importantly, Ruan's algae can not only be used to produce fuel, but can also clean up the wastewater, potentially saving millions of dollars.

"That's what we're after," says Jason Willet, finance director for Metropolitan Council Environmental Services, which operates the wastewater plant and has helped fund Ruan's research.

A single acre of algae, even in an inefficient open pond, can produce 5,000 gallons of biodiesel per year, says Ruan— 100 times as much as soybeans. And unlike many other algal biofuel experiments, Ruan's work does not rely on food-based crops, such as sugar cane, as a feedstock to produce the algae.

"This (sewage-based biofuel) potentially is a very, very good energy crop," says Ruan, a professor of biosystems and agricultural engineering. "Potentially its yield can be much, much higher than starch from corn or oil from soybeans. The main reason is that it can grow at a much, much faster rate."

Growing Interest in Biofuel

Growing fuel-producing algae in waste is not Ruan's idea alone. The concept drew international attention in 2006 when a startup in New Zealand called Aquaflow successfully harvested biofuel from open-air ponds at wastewater treatment plants. The company expects to be able to produce the biofuel on a large scale, and recently attracted the attention of major players in the airline industry by announcing it had distilled a special blend that meets the technical specifications for jet fuel.

Aquaflow's advances, combined with the Pentagon's interest in biofuels as an alternative to conventional jetfuels, has sparked a flurry of academic and industrial research in the United States. A team at the University of Virginia has been working to maximize the efficiency of the algae-growing process, and the chemistry department at Old Dominion University in Norfolk, Va., has built a small-scale bioreactor at a local wastewater treatment plant that may eventually be able to produce $600,000 worth of fuel per year.

Even NASA [the National Aeronautics and Space Administration] has thrown its hat in the ring, with researchers working on the development of floating greenhouses for algae cultivation. The bags are stocked with human waste and sown with species of freshwater algae, and then deployed into the ocean. The semi-porous plastic membrane allows the exchange of CO_2 and oxygen to continue uninhibited, but prevents the salty seawater from disturbing the fecund growing conditions inside. Soaking up the sun and feasting on the nutrients in the sewage, the algae produce fat-laden cells that can be harvested and refined into fuels.

U.S. entrepreneurs have also entered the market. In June [2009], Indianapolis-based Algaewheel contracted with the city of Reynolds, Ind., to construct a module at a wastewater treatment facility that uses a wheel-like rotating contraption to filter incoming sewage through a series of algae cultures. The fuel generated from the process will be used to power the facility.

Cleaner Water and Biofuel

In Minneapolis, Ruan and the Metro Council are conducting research with the intention of designing a demonstration algae-to-fuel plant within about a year.

The Metropolitan Wastewater Treatment Plant sits beside the Mississippi River, just downstream from St Paul. The 10th-largest plant of its kind in the country, it treats sewage from three-fourths of the Twin Cities metro area—more than 200 million gallons a day. Some of its low brick buildings, adorned by graceful Art Deco lettering, date to the plant's origin in 1938. From a rooftop, the 170-acre grounds is a warren of basins, tanks, stacks, and pipes.

The university was looking for a way to produce a renewable fuel that wouldn't compete with food crops.

Incoming sewage is screened for trash and chunks, then runs into settling ponds to remove solids. In aeration ponds, carefully managed populations of microbes break down organics. After more settling to remove dead microbes, wastewater is sterilized with liquid chlorine before being discharged into the river. The effluent is often cleaner and clearer than the river itself. Amazingly, there is barely a whiff of odor.

As clean as the effluent is, Minnesota is considering new standards that will most likely require further reduction of phosphorous and nitrogen. Excess phosphorus is a real concern in the land of 10,000 Lakes because it causes unsightly algae blooms and fish kills. Nitrogen sluicing off farmland throughout the Midwest is blamed for the hypoxic dead zone at the Mississippi River's mouth. But meeting the new standards through conventional treatment could easily cost "hundreds of million of dollars" a year, says Willet. "We need to find some options."

So the University of Minnesota and the Met Council began research in 2007. Through its Initiative for Renewable Energy and the Environment, the university was looking for a way to produce a renewable fuel that wouldn't compete with food crops or tie up agricultural land. The Met Council wanted cleaner wastewater.

Refining the Biofuel Process

Early on, Ruan decided against growing algae on the raw wastewater streaming into the plant: The task of managing more than 200 million gallons a day seemed daunting. Instead, research focused on the "centrate," the millions of gallons squeezed from settling-pond solids by powerful centrifuges. The foul juice is so high in nitrogen and phosphorus that it kills most organisms.

Ruan's initial task was to screen thousands of species of algae to find one, or several, that would flourish in the harsh conditions of the centrate. He dispatched his assistants to scoop green, soupy water from ponds and rivers. Most perished in the concentrated nutrients, but Ruan eventually found several species—greenish, spherical, single-celled plankton only 5 microns across—that survived. By acclimating these survivors, Ruan was able to produce strains that thrived in the wastewater, while reducing the levels of phosphorus by 50 to 80 percent. They yielded 30 percent of their mass as oil and grew so fast they could be harvested daily.

So far Ruan and the Met Council have shunned genetically engineered algae, though they almost certainly could boost growth and oil content. "We are not interested because eventually on a massive operation like this, some of it is going to get loose in the river," says Willet. "And I have enough regulations."

Ruan also decided against open ponds to grow his algae. Ponds are inefficient, because algae blooms block light. Commercial-scale ponds would also require large acreage, and conditions are tough to control, especially in winter. "If you're talking about an open pond system, it's almost impossible in a northern climate," says Ruan. Finally, "if the algae is dilute, it's very, very expensive to harvest it."

Instead, Ruan began building dozens of different "photobioreactors"—various configurations of tubes or plates that allow good exposure to natural and artificial light, as well as easy access for harvesting and cleaning. The current generation of reactors is operating in a shed in the plant's "solids building," not only to contain the stench of the centrate, but also to keep the equipment secret until the university secures patents.

Like soybeans, algae oil can be used to make biodiesel. Or it can be "cracked" through heat and catalysts (as in an oil refinery) to produce "green diesel," identical to petroleum-derived diesel. Either biodiesel or green diesel could power the Metro Council's public bus fleet, which already uses biodiesel in blends of up to 20 percent. "We are a guaranteed market," says Willet, Remnant algae mash—the nitrogen-rich pulp—can be sold as fertilizer, animal feed, or raw material for ethanol.

Harvesting Biofuel

But there's one big problem, Ruan says, and it's common to any attempt to convert algae to fuel. "We have done a lot of work to get the oil out, but we know it is expensive," says Ruan, who is lead scientist on several other promising algae biofuel projects that do not use wastewater as a feedstock.

Two methods are in common use: Drying and crushing the algae, or removing oil with a solvent. Both, says Ruan, are expensive. Researchers are exploring various ways to break down algae cell walls—through osmotic shock or ultrasound, for example—to make oil recovery easier.

That is the key—wastewater treatment with the added benefit of renewable energy. Or renewable fuel with the benefit of cleaner water.

It pays to keep trying, because with available processes, Ruan says, algae-diesel might cost $20 a gallon. But, says Willet, "that doesn't take into account the avoided costs that I will realize."

During the next year, Ruan and the Met Council hope to develop a design for a demonstration-scale plant to utilize perhaps 20,000 gallons of centrate a day. That amount is only 2 percent of the centrate the Metro plant generates, and would produce only about 160 kilograms of dry algae and 8 gallons of oil a day. But, says Ruan, an algae plant of that size could eventually be scaled up to treat the entire stream of centrate and produce near 400 gallons of oil a day. Or it could be used as is to treat the wastewater of a city of 50,000 people.

And that is the key—wastewater treatment with the added benefit of renewable fuel. Or renewable fuel with the benefit of cleaner water. Either way, says Ruan, "we feel that this is probably a perfect combination."

8

Using Human Waste for Energy Is Problematic

Una

Una is a writer for the Straight Dope, a popular, question-and-answer style syndicated newspaper column and website.

In history, it has been common to get rid of human waste by burning it; it has also been common to use human waste as fuel. Today, however, the process of burning human waste and using it as fuel is complicated by what is dumped into sewage systems. Everything from dishwashing soaps from households to heavy metals from factories are filtered through the system. As a result, burning raw sewage has the potential to create toxic fumes. Another problem is that sewage, treated or nontreated, is not very efficient as a fuel. As a resource for power, then, sewage cannot compete with most other options.

The waste products of most animals can be used as fuel, and likely have been at one time or another. This isn't just in so-called primitive cultures, either—many technologically modern nations have studied and implemented both animal and human waste combustion.

Although you might wonder why anyone would burn hippopotamus manure or human waste given the many other fuel sources available, two very good reasons drive their utilization. First, animal and human waste is generally considered a renewable energy source and thus can be burned as "green power," giving the entity combusting the waste (as well as the country in which it resides) a political or treaty-fulfilling credit for reducing greenhouse-gas emissions. Second, some cities and regions have limited landfill or wastewater treatment capacity, and burning the waste can reduce the load on their waste disposal facilities. Other benefits from burning these waste products can include tax credits for using renewable energy sources and good public relations karma. Still another benefit is that burning animal waste can prevent its decomposition into methane, a greenhouse gas that's much worse for the environment than carbon dioxide.

Everything dumped down the drain, both at home and at factories, ends up in the sewage treatment system.

Burning Sewage Sludge Is Dangerous

That said, waste combustion presents some significant problems, and one of my many jobs is assessing just what those problems are, the degree of risk involved, and what can be done to minimize the risk.

Human waste combustion needs to be discussed separately from animal waste because the human variety is more hazardous to burn, although not for the reason you might imagine, namely the potential spread of disease or parasites. Outside of college pranks or conceptual art exhibits, few seriously consider burning human waste in its original state. Instead, what we're almost always talking about is burning sewage sludge, the dewatered mass of organic and other compounds produced by sewage treatment plants. The problem is that everything dumped down the drain, both at home and at factories, ends up in the sewage treatment system. This includes household soaps and chemicals, industrial oils and solvents, heavy metals such as mercury and cadmium, and even some mildly radioactive materials. While some fraction of these is separated out during the sewage treatment process, and other items decay or de-volatize, much of the stuff ends up in the sludge.

As you can imagine, burning sewage sludge will release many of these toxins into the environment. Even the best emissions control systems can't remove all the heavy metals, dioxins, and other unpleasant items from the gases going up the smokestack. Whether sludge combustion is more hazardous than, say, coal combustion depends on the specific properties of the sludge, but the thing is, there's more to it than just throwing another buffalo chip on the fire. In the United States sewage sludge typically isn't considered an "opportunity fuel" unless it has a minimal level of hazardous materials. Even then, a driver such as a lack of landfill space or tax incentives of Biblical proportions is generally needed to make it feasible.

Using Sewage Sludge for Fuel

Determining to what extent sewage sludge is used as fuel is a challenge. The European Commission estimates that in 2005 approximately 21% of the sludge produced by its member countries was incinerated. Most of this wasn't used for power production, however, and was incinerated simply to dispose of it. In the United States, sewage sludge combustion is uncommon, and is even more rarely used for power generation—the only reliable figures I've been able to find are for 2002, when approximately 0.007% of total electric power production came from sewage sludge combustion. I can tell you from personal experience that while many U.S. utilities have considered sewage sludge combustion, the fear of increased heavy metal (mainly mercury) and dioxin emissions has shut down all the sewage sludge projects I've worked on.

Unlike humans, animals generally don't have a convenient centralized waste collection system (highly-trained toilet-using cats excepted). That means the animal waste fuel supply is often afflicted with low "energy density," a frequent problem with alternative fuel sources. Unlike fossil fuel and some biomass resources, animal and human waste often requires substantial ongoing investment in collection and transportation in order to achieve economies of scale. For example, while a single farm may produce a score or more tons of cow manure per day, a typical coal power plant burns 500 tons of coal an hour. Add to this the fact that for some processes there's just no practical way to collect the waste and prepare it for transport to the power facility. A small-scale plant can be located near a convenient supply, but opportunities for these are limited, and small-scale plants typically are expensive for what you get.

Another problem common to all animal (and human) waste is its unsuitability as a fuel. Manure generally has a high moisture content when first produced, and this moisture must be removed by either drying in the environment or industrial drying. Drying in the environment involves noxious emissions and a lot of time, while industrial drying requires energy, which can reduce the efficiency of the system below the break-even point. Even after the waste is dried, its heat output is typically poorer than the worst coal commercially available.

In case you were wondering, the heat content of human waste is highly variable due mostly to its moisture content, which can be 90% or more *in situ* [in its natural state] and is often still 50–75% after pressing and vacuuming. When totally dry, sewage sludge has about 4000–7000 Btu/lb, which is equivalent in heat to lignite coal—also, appropriately, called "brown coal." On a wet basis, it can have less than 1000 Btu/lb, which is too little to sustain its own combustion.

9

All Diapers Have an Environmental Impact

Michael McDonough

Michael McDonough is a writer for the Associated Press.

Over the past several years a debate has raged: Which diaper, cloth or disposable, has the greatest impact on the environment? Settling the argument of which diaper is the best is difficult. Disposable diapers are convenient but are discarded into landfills. Cloth diapers, on the other hand, need to be washed, requiring a great deal of water. Neither option is a clear-cut superior choice. All diapers have an environmental impact and are a matter of individual choice.

Disposable diapers, most of which end up in landfill sites in Britain, have the same environmental impact as reusable diapers, when the effect of laundering the cotton version is taken into account, Britain's environmental watchdog said Thursday.

Makers of disposable diapers—known as nappies in Britain—welcomed the findings published by the Environment Agency, saying parents should no longer feel guilty about using their products.

But advocates of reusable diapers, who have built up a fledgling network of cotton nappy users in recent years, including laundry services that collect dirty diapers and provide clean ones, said the study was flawed.

The Environment Agency said an independent consultant carried out a three-year study that assessed all the environmental impacts of the two kinds of diaper. That included the raw materials used to make them—down to the crude oil from which chemicals are extracted to produce disposable diapers—as well as transport costs, means of use and disposal, and the energy required throughout the life cycle of the diaper.

The main impact from cotton diapers came from the electricity and fuel used when washing and drying them.

The study found there was "no substantial difference between the environmental impacts" of using disposable and reusable diapers, said Tricia Henton, director of environmental protection at the Environment Agency.

The agency said disposable diapers accounted for 2.5 percent of Britain's annual household waste. British parents bought some 2.5 billion disposable diapers in 2001, and most of them ended up in landfill sites. They held a 94 percent share of the British diaper market in 1999.

"We hope manufacturers of disposable nappies will use this study to improve the environmental performance of their products, particularly the quantities going to landfill," Henton said.

The Environment Agency said the main impact from cotton diapers came from the electricity and fuel used when washing and drying them. Henton said parents should wash them in bigger loads at lower temperatures and dry them in fresh air.

Impact of Diapers

Around 675,000 children are born each year in Britain. On average they wear diapers until they are 2 years and 2 months old. Disposable diapers first appeared in Britain in the 1960s and were quickly embraced by parents as a means of reducing their laundry workload. But in recent years concerns have grown about their environmental consequences.

Tracy Stewart, director general of the Absorbent Hygiene Products Manufacturers' Association, welcomed the Environment Agency's findings.

"Parents can be thrilled by the news and no longer feel guilty about choosing disposables," she said.

Stewart acknowledged there was little alternative in Britain to disposing of the diapers in landfill sites, but she insisted that 80 percent of a used disposable diaper is biodegradable.

Green campaigners, however, sharply criticized the official study.

The Women's Environment Network said the sample size relied on for assessing the habits of cotton diaper users was too small for any solid conclusions to be drawn.

Spokeswoman Elizabeth Hartigan said parents could make a big difference by using energy efficient washing machines and laundering diapers at lower temperatures—around 60° C.

"People who are using real nappies can save waste using them and be confident they're not harming the environment by using energy to wash them," Hartigan told British Broadcasting Corp. radio.

Responding to Hartigan's criticism, Henton said the Environment Agency would carry out further work to verify its study. She said getting a big sample of cotton diaper users was difficult as only about 5 percent of parents fitted into that category.

10

Diapers Are Unnecessary

AP Online

AP Online is a part of the Associated Press, an American news agency.

In recent years, debate has raged over whether parents should use cloth or disposable diapers. More recently, a third option has presented itself: allowing babies to go diaper free. By paying attention to certain behavior cues, the parent will be able to sense when a child needs to eliminate. This is more hygienic for the baby and environmentally friendly due to the fact that diapers are no longer being used. While going diaper free may seem like a shocking step for parents, proponents believe the rewards are considerable.

Thirteen-month-old Dominic Klatt stopped banging the furniture in the verandah, looked at his mother and clasped his right hand around his left wrist to signal that he needed to go to the bathroom.

His mother took the diaper-less tot to a tree in the yard, held him in a squatting position and made a gentle hissing sound—prompting the infant to relieve himself on cue before he rushed back to play.

Dominic is a product of a growing "diaper-free" movement founded on the belief that babies are born with an instinctive ability to signal when they have to answer nature's call. Parents who practice the so-called "elimination communication" learn to read their children's body language to help them recognize the need, and they mimic the sounds that a child associates with the bathroom.

Erinn Klatt began toilet training her son at birth and said he has not wet his bed at night since he was six months old.

"The nice part is . . . really getting the majority of poops in the toilet versus having to clean that," Klatt said. "I don't have to wake up at night and change diapers or have wet sheets anywhere. That's really nice.

"And being able to travel without a big, bloated diaper bag is terrific," she said.

Diaper-Free Infants

Some parents and toilet training experts are skeptical.

"They teach them from birth? Oh, my God!" said 40-year-old Lisa Bolcato, as she held her 5-month-old daughter, Rose, at a park on Boston Common. "When you're getting two hours of sleep between feedings, I don't think that you have the time to do it. You just make sure that your child's healthy and happy and well-fed."

Some parents begin going diaper-free at birth, and the infants can initiate bowel movements on cue as young as 3 to 4 months.

Still, the practice is common in many parts of rural Africa and Asia where parents cannot afford diapers.

In the United States, many of the parents are stay-at-home-moms, but there are also working mothers. Some meet in on-line groups, at homes and in public parks to share experiences and cheer each others' efforts.

Experts at the Child Study Center at the University of Oklahoma Health Sciences Center say children younger than 12 months have no control over bladder or bowel movements and little control for 6 months after that.

But some parents begin going diaper-free at birth, and the infants can initiate bowel movements on cue as young as 3 to 4 months, said Elizabeth Parise, spokeswoman of Diaper FreeBaby.org, a network of free support groups promoting the practice.

And unlike some methods of toilet training, there are no rewards or punishment associated with it.

Dr. Mark Wolraich, professor of pediatrics and director of the Child Study Center, said the practice essentially conditions young children to go to the bathroom at predictable times or show clear signs when they must go.

"To be truly toilet-trained, the child has to be able to have the sensation that they need to go, be able to interpret that sensation and be able to then tell the parent and take some action," said Wolraich, who is also editor of the American Academy of Pediatrics' book on toilet training.

"And that's different from reading the subtle signs that the child is making when they have to go to the bathroom."

The practice also enables parents to get insight into an infant's development since more accidents occur if a child falls sick or enters a new phase such as learning to crawl, walk or talk.

Forging Closer Ties

Parents attempt the early training to forge closer ties with their infants, to reduce the environmental impact associated with diapers and to avoid skin irritation caused by a wet diaper, Parise said.

Others were inspired by observing the practice while traveling abroad.

The practice also enables parents to get insight into an infant's development since more accidents occur if a child falls sick or enters a new phase such as learning to crawl, walk or talk.

This is because an infant may be too distracted by illness or efforts to master a new skill to communicate the need to go to the bathroom, said Melinda Rothstein, an MIT [Massachusetts Institute of Technology] business school graduate who co-founded DiaperFreeBaby.org.

She says finding a supportive daycare center is the biggest challenge for parents who choose not to use diapers. Other problems include finding tiny underwear for diaper-free infants.

Isis Arnesen, 33, of Boston, has a 14-week-old daughter, Lucia, who is diaper-free. She said it can be awkward to explain the process to people, such as when she helped Lucia relieve herself in a sink at a public restroom.

"Sometimes I don't know what's gonna happen and it doesn't work, and sometimes I feel a little embarrassed," Arnesen said. "It makes her happy though, right? She smiles, she's happy."

11

Human Waste Still Divides Castes in India

Andrew Buncombe

Andrew Buncombe is a writer for the British newspaper the In-dependent, *covering India, Pakistan, Burma, Nepal, and Bangladesh.*

In India, the practice of manual scavenging—in which poor Indians clean the latrines of wealthier Indians—has been treated as a cultural tradition. While the Indian government has attempted to end the practice, many members of the lowest caste, the "untouchables," or Dalits, continue the practice. One person, however, has begun a crusade to put an end to manual scavenging. Bezwada Wilson, whose parents were manual scavengers, formed Safai Karmachari Andolan (SKA) for that purpose. SKA, a group actively involved in destroying illegal latrines and rehabilitating scavengers, has dedicated itself to ending manual scavenging in India.

There is an infectious, impassioned enthusiasm about Bezwada Wilson that is hard to ignore. He laughs, he smiles. He frowns too, but soon he is smiling again. And yet things might have been very different. When he was aged 18, he came very close to taking his own life. The thing that led him to the very edge was the discovery of what his parents really did to scrape together a living.

Growing up in a gold mining area of southern India, they had told him as a child that they mined for ore. The evening they revealed to him that they were actually "dry latrine" cleaners who spent their days covered in the filth of others, he was so horrified, so disgusted, that he came close to committing suicide at a secluded water tower. After hours of weeping, wrestling with his thoughts, he decided he was better off alive, fighting to help people like his parents.

Two decades later, his efforts have been nothing short of remarkable. As head of a nationwide organisation that has confronted head-on some of his country's most ingrained prejudice, he believes he is close to eradicating the dehumanising practice known as "manual scavenging".

Ending Manual Scavenging

Ten years ago [in 2000], there were around three million people employed as manual scavengers in India; today there are fewer than 600,000. By the end of the year [2010], he believes the figure will be zero. "Once people realise that it's slavery, they want to stop. The problem is that it's never discussed publicly," Mr Wilson said.

Dry latrines are toilets that do not flush. In most Indian homes, such latrines have been replaced with flush systems. In 1993, a law ruled all dry latrines should be destroyed and the practice of manual scavenging abolished. But in pockets of India, especially in poorer states such as Uttar Pradesh, Rajasthan and Bihar, the practice has persisted.

The work of a scavenger is filthy and soul-destroying.

In India, the people employed to clean such toilets have always been members of groups of "Untouchable" or Dalit people. Equipped with nothing more sophisticated than a brush and bucket or pieces of cardboard, such groups have cleaned the toilets of higher-caste people, carrying away the waste, or "nightsoil", in baskets placed on their heads.

Payment for such work is minimal; many scavengers say they do it because they have always done so, because their parents and grandparents did the same. Activists say it is a form of bondage.

The work of a scavenger is filthy and soul-destroying. One morning I accompanied two women, members of the Balmiki clan, as they went about their work on the edge of the city of Ambala, in Haryana.

The Daily Life of a Scavenger

Cheranji Kaur and Seema clean six dry latrines every morning, using a brush to sweep away the waste into a nearby open drain. "I started this work at the age of 10," said 35-year-old Mrs Kaur. "My parents did it, our ancestors did it. I'd go with my parents; that is how you learn."

The women made their way around a scruffy, higher-caste neighbourhood where they set about cleaning the toilets. One resident threw a bucket of water into the latrine, sending the waste splashing and gushing as the two women used their brushes to clean it away. The air was sour and corrosive. It was a sad sight, made worse by the women's determination to try to retain their dignity as they worked, and keep their clothes clean, gold bangles bouncing on their wrists.

One of the latrines belonged to a family of Sikhs, a religion whose founder utterly rejected the notion of caste differences. The head of the household, Mahinder Singh, said he paid the women 50 rupees (71p) a month and that "it had always been the Balmiki who cleaned the toilets".

Mr Singh added: "Everybody gets it done so we get it done. Those who are supposed to do it, should do it. I did not know it was illegal."

Mr Wilson's campaign has two aims: to raise awareness among groups of scavengers that they do not have to perform such tasks, and then help them find alternative work. A key element of his publicity drives, or yatras, is the symbolic burning of the scavengers' wooden baskets and the destruction of the dry latrines themselves.

In one incident in the southern state of Andhra Pradesh, activists discovered a block of supposedly outlawed dry latrines in a court complex, which were being used by judges. When activists destroyed the toilets, officials did not dare protest, aware that the existence of the latrines had been in breach of the law.

Mrs Kaur and Seema revealed that they laboured every day for around 150 rupees a month. They said the work was difficult, it was hard to get rid of the smell and they suffered widespread discrimination.

"We do it because there is no other work," said Mrs Kaur, who has two young children. "The other communities will not let us inside their homes to work as cleaners or domestic servants. Any work would be better than this; a little shop, a vegetable cart, or rearing cattle."

Seema added: "I don't feel good doing this work, people look at us different, they look down at us."

Rehabilitating Scavengers

Largely as a result of the work of Mr Wilson and his group Safai Karmachari Andolan (SKA), there are now just a handful of scavengers in the state of Haryana. One of those who was "rehabilitated" is Saroj Balla. She had worked as a scavenger all her life to earn enough to send her children to school. Thirty years ago, members of her community even struggled to buy vegetables; vendors would put them on the floor rather than hand them over directly.

Once, when Mrs Balla was pregnant, she fell from a ladder while descending from a dry latrine located on a roof, collapsing on the floor in a slew of human waste. The toilet owners refused to help her, instead prodding her with a stick to make her get to her feet.

Five years ago, activists from SKA, which receives support and some funding from Christian Aid, which is based in London, arrived in Ambala and told Mrs Balla and others that they were not required to perform such degrading work. "They told us we had a right to a better life," Mrs Balla said, her voice swelling. "We all knew it was dirty work. We took courage from the people who came to talk with us."

The 50-year-old recalled the day that she and other scavengers went out and demolished 15 dry latrines in the area. The toilets' owners had told them to clean them, but instead the group of women used heavy sticks to break them up. "I felt very good," said Mrs Balla, who now works as a domestic help. "It felt like a rebirth" Her advice to the other two women was simple: definitely stop.

Mr Wilson, 44, who presented a piece of brick from a demolished dry latrine to Navi Pillay, the UN High Commissioner for Human Rights, talks about eradicating all scavenging by 31 December of this year [2010]. Volunteers are currently holding rallies across the country and will descend on [India's capital city] Delhi at the end of the month.

By then he believes the number of people working as scavengers will have been reduced from 600,000 to 300,000, giving him two months to finish his task.

"Everything is messed up. People say we are unclean, but who has made us unclean? We are cleaners; the person shitting in a dry latrine is the dirty person," he said. "For thousands of years we have been told we are dirty. Now people are shouting back, 'No, we are not dirty.'"

12

Human Waste Disposal in the Backcountry Presents Challenges

Leave No Trace Center for Outdoor Ethics

Leave No Trace Center for Outdoor Ethics is a nonprofit educational organization dedicated to responsible enjoyment of the outdoors.

With millions of people hiking on trails in the backcountry each year, the disposal of human waste has become a major issue. While burying human feces is the correct manner of disposal in most locations, solid waste must be packed out from certain places. Digging catholes and latrines are just some of the ways a person can properly dispose of human waste in the backcountry. A "leave no trace" mentality, in which waste is packed out and in which the person leaves the campsite, hiking trail, etc., just as it was found is to be encouraged.

Proper disposal of human waste is important to avoid pollution of water sources, avoid the negative implications of someone else finding it, minimize the possibility of spreading disease, and maximize the rate of decomposition.

In most locations, burying human feces in the correct manner is the most effective method to meet these criteria. Solid human waste must be packed out from some places, such as narrow river canyons. Land management agencies can advise you of specific rules for the area you plan to visit.

Contrary to popular opinion, research indicates that burial of feces actually slows decomposition (at least in the Rocky Mountains). Pathogens have been discovered to survive for a year or more when buried. However, in light of the other problems associated with feces, it is still generally best to bury it. The slow decomposition rate causes the need to choose the correct location, far from water, campsites, and other frequently used places.

Catholes

Catholes are the most widely accepted method of waste disposal. Locate catholes at least 200 feet (about 70 adult steps) from water, trails and camp. Select an inconspicuous site where other people will be unlikely to walk or camp. With a small garden trowel, dig a hole 6–8 inches deep and 4–6 inches in diameter. The cathole should be covered and disguised with natural materials when finished. If camping in the area for more than one night, or if camping with a large group, cathole sites should be widely dispersed. . . .

The advantages [of catholes] are:

- They are easy to dig in most areas.

- They are easy to disguise after use.

- They are private.

- They disperse the waste rather than concentrate it (which enhances decomposition).

- it is usually easy to select an out of the way location where you can be certain no one is going to casually encounter the cathole. . . .

A cathole is the most widely accepted means of waste disposal in arid lands. Locate catholes at least 200 feet (about 70 adult steps) from water, trails, and camp. Avoid areas where water visibly flows, such as sandy washes, even if they are dry at the moment. Select a site that will maximize exposure to the sun in order to aid decomposition. Because the sun's heat will penetrate desert soils several inches, it can eventually kill pathogens if the feces are buried properly. South-facing slopes and ridge tops will have more exposure to sun and heat than other areas.

Placing toilet paper in plastic bags and packing it out as trash is the best way to Leave No Trace in a desert environment.

Latrines

Though catholes are recommended for most situations, there are times when latrines may be more applicable, such as when camping with young children or if staying in one camp for longer than a few nights. Use similar criteria for selecting a latrine location as those used to locate a cathole. Since this higher concentration of feces will decompose very slowly, location is especially important. A good way to speed decomposition and diminish odors is to toss in a handful of soil after each use. Ask your land manager about latrine-building techniques.

Use toilet paper sparingly and use only plain, white, nonperfumed brands. Toilet paper must be disposed of properly! It should either be thoroughly buried in a cathole or placed in plastic bags and packed out. Natural toilet paper has been used by many campers for years. When done correctly, this method is as sanitary as regular toilet paper, but without the [environmental] impact problems. Popular types of natural toilet paper include stones, vegetation and snow. Obviously, some experimentation is necessary to make this practice work for you, but it is worth a try! Burning toilet paper in a cathole is not generally recommended.

Toilet Paper in Arid Lands: Placing toilet paper in plastic bags and packing it out as trash is the best way to Leave No

Trace in a desert environment. Toilet paper should not be burned. This practice can result in wild fires.

Tampons

Proper disposal of tampons requires that they be placed in plastic bags and packed out. Do not bury them because they don't decompose readily and animals may dig them up. It will take a very hot, intense fire to burn them completely.

Urine

Urine has little direct effect on vegetation or soil. In some instances urine may draw wildlife, which are attracted to the salts. They can defoliate plants and dig up soil. Urinating on rocks, pine needles, and gravel is less likely to attract wildlife. Diluting urine with water from a water bottle can help minimize negative effects.

Special Considerations for River Canyons

River canyons often present unique Leave No Trace problems. The most common practice is to urinate directly in[to] the river and pack out feces in sealed boxes for later disposal. Check with your land manager for details about specific areas.

Organizations to Contact

The editors have compiled the following list of organizations concerned with the issues debated in this book. The descriptions are derived from materials provided by the organizations. All have publications or information available for interested readers. The list was compiled on the date of publication of the present volume; names, addresses, phone and fax numbers, and e-mail and Internet addresses may change. Be aware that many organizations take several weeks or longer to respond to inquiries, so allow as much time as possible.

Centers for Disease Control and Prevention (CDC)
1600 Clifton Rd., Atlanta, GA   30333
(800) 232-4636
website: www.cdc.gov

The CDC is the primary government organization that monitors diseases and threats to the nation's health and advises the public on disease prevention at home, in the workplace, and elsewhere. The CDC website provides access to information on health issues, including the reports "Guidance for Controlling Potential Risks to Workers Exposed to Class B Biosolids" and "Guidance for Reducing Health Risks to Workers Handling Human Waste or Sewage."

Clean Water Action
1010 Vermont Ave. NW, Suite 400
Washington, DC   20005-4918
(202) 895-0420 • fax: (202) 895-0438
e-mail: cwa@cleanwater.org
website: www.cleanwateraction.org

Clean Water Action is a grassroots organization that works to empower people to take action to protect America's waters, build healthy communities, and make democracy work for everyone. Clean Water Action's national campaigns work to impact federal laws and policy, while state offices focus on local concerns. One of Clean Water Action's primary methods of increasing public awareness is its door-to-door campaigns on issues such as water pollution, global warming, the energy economy, and building healthy communities. Several reports, summaries, fact sheets, and other materials are available on Clean Water Action's website.

IRC International Water and Sanitation Centre
PO Box 82327, The Hague   2508 EH
   The Netherlands
+31 70 304-4000 • fax: +31 70 304-4044
e-mail: www.irc.nl/page/5751
website: www.irc.nl

The IRC International Water and Sanitation Centre was established by the World Health Organization in 1968 to facilitate the sharing, promotion, and use of knowledge so that governments, professionals, and organizations can better support people in developing countries to obtain water and sanitation services that they will use and maintain. The IRC is staffed with internationally recognized specialists and dedicated support staff working in a variety of fields of importance to the water and sanitation sector. The IRC Source Water and Sanitation News Service publishes the *Source Features and Source Bulletin*, which comes out four times per year, and an electronic newsletter, the *Source Weekly*, which is issued twenty times per year.

National Solid Wastes Management Association (NSWMA)
4301 Connecticut Ave. NW, Suite 300, Washington, DC   20008
(202) 244-4700 • fax: (202) 966-4824
e-mail: membership@envasns.org
website: www.nswma.org

Founded in 1962, NSWMA is a trade association that represents for-profit companies that provide waste collection, recycling, and disposal services. Its goal is to promote environmentally responsible and ethical waste management.

Publications on its website include research bulletins, "Profiles in Garbage" fact sheets, the monthly magazine *Waste Age*, and a detailed outline of the history of waste management.

Natural Resources Defense Council (NRDC)

40 W. Twentieth St., New York, NY   10011
(212) 727-2700 • fax: (212) 727-1773
e-mail: nrdcinfo@nrdc.org
website: www.nrdc.org

The Natural Resources Defense Council is an environmental group of lawyers and scientists who help write environmental laws and seek to protect the quality of land, air, and water. The NRDC conducts research into topics such as cleaning up the oceans and removing toxic chemicals from the environment. NRDC publishes the quarterly magazine *OnEarth*, a monthly e-mail newsletter, and reports on environmental issues, including *Testing the Waters 2010: A Guide to Water Quality at Vacation Beaches*.

Sierra Club

85 Second St., 2nd Floor, San Francisco, CA   94105-3441
(415) 977-5500 • fax: (415) 977-5799
e-mail: information@sierraclub.org
website: www.sierraclub.org

Founded in 1892, the Sierra Club is a grassroots organization that promotes the protection and conservation of natural resources. The organization maintains separate committees on air quality, global environment, and solid waste, among other environmental concerns, to help achieve its goals. It publishes books, fact sheets, the bimonthly magazine *Sierra*, and the *Planet* newsletter, which appears several times a year.

US Environmental Protection Agency (EPA)

1200 Pennsylvania Ave. NW, Washington, DC   20460
(202) 272-0167
website: www.epa.gov

The EPA is the government agency charged with protecting human health and safeguarding the natural environment. It works to protect Americans from environmental health risks, enforce federal environmental regulations, and ensure that environmental protection is an integral consideration in US policy. The EPA publishes many reports, fact sheets, and educational materials, including "Land Application of Sewage Sludge" and "Biosolids: Frequently Asked Questions." Within the EPA, the Office of Solid Waste and Emergency Response provides policy, guidance, and direction for the agency's emergency response and waste programs.

Water for People
6666 W. Quincy Ave., Denver, CO   80235
(303) 734-3490 • fax: (303) 734-3499
e-mail: info@waterforpeople.org
website: www.waterforpeople.org

Water for People helps people in developing countries improve their quality of life by supporting the development of locally sustainable drinking water resources, sanitation facilities, and health and hygiene education programs. The organization hopes to see a world where all people have access to safe drinking water and sanitation and where no one suffers or dies from a water- or sanitation-related disease. Water for People publishes a quarterly newsletter, *Connections*, as well as various special reports and a series of audiocasts called *Voices from the Field*.

Bibliography

Books

Jamie Benidickson and Graeme Wynn | *The Culture of Flushing: A Social and Legal History of Sewage.* Vancouver: University of British Columbia Press, 2007.

Maggie Black and Ben Fawcett | *The Last Taboo: Opening the Door on the Global Sanitation Crisis.* London: Earthscan, 2008.

W. Hodding Carter | *Flushed: How the Plumber Saved Civilization.* New York: Atria, 2006.

Rose George | *The Big Necessity: The Unmentionable World of Human Waste and Why It Matters.* New York: Henry Holt, 2009.

L. Julie Horn | *The Porcelain God: A Social History of the Toilet.* New York: Citadel, 2000.

Joseph Jenkins | *The Humanure Handbook: A Guide to Composting Human Manure.* 3rd ed. Grove City, PA: Jenkins, 2005.

Shepard Krech III | *The Ecological Indian: Myth and History.* New York: Norton, 1999.

Martin V. Melosi | *The Sanitary City: Environmental Services in Urban America from Colonial Times to the Present.* Pittsburgh: University of Pittsburgh Press, 2008.

Laura Noren and Harvey Molotch, eds.	*Toilet: Public Restrooms and the Politics of Sharing*. New York: New York University Press, 2010.
Dave Praeger	*Poop Culture: How America Is Shaped by Its Grossest National Product*. Los Angeles: Feral House, 2007.

Periodicals and Internet Sources

Valerie Boog	"Drinking Our Waste," *Swiss News*, November 2010.
Chip Cutter	"Foul Smells and Plenty of Ick: Port-a-Potty Cleaner, It's Not a Crappy Job," *Indianapolis Business Journal*, July 14, 2008.
Alistair Driver	"Soil Association Wants Human Waste to Be Spread on Farmland," *Farmers Guardian*, November 29, 2010. www.farmersguardian.com.
Ben Fawcett	"Making More than Mention of an Unmentionable Crisis," *Water and Wastewater International*, vol. 24, no.2, 2009.
Federal Register	"Hazardous Waste Management System; Identification and Listing of Hazardous Waste; Proposed Rule," January 28, 2011.
Bill McKibben	"Hazardous Material: Warning! This Review Contains Explicit Language Referring to Human Waste. Handle with Care," *Books & Culture*, January–February 2009.

Mohammed Omer	"Raw Sewage Runs in the Streets of Gaza," *National Catholic Reporter*, March 7, 2008.
Patrick Raleigh	"Flushing for Fuel," *Process Engineering*, November 23, 2010.
Skills Ahead	"Impacts of Solid Waste on Human Health," November 1, 2010.
Gar Smith	"Solving the Water and Energy Crisis—in One Swell Poop," *Earth Island Journal*, Winter 2010.
Carol Steinfeld	"You Can Compost Human Waste!," *Mother Earth News*, April–May 2011.
Rachel Taylor	"Making a Natural Impact," *Ecos*, June–July 2006.
Mari Marcel Thekaekara	"A Lifetime in Muck," *New Internationalist*, August 2008.
Siobhan Wagner	"Human Waste Powers VW Beetle," *Engineer*, August 6, 2010.
Waste & Recycling News	"Endless Source; North Carolina Wastewater Plant to Convert Human Waste to Energy," November 2010.
Kirsten Weir	"What a Waste: Billions of People Around the World Lack Proper Sanitation," *Current Science: A Weekly Reader Publication*, October 2009.

Index